# Joining the Literacy Club

*Further Essays into Education*

FRANK SMITH

*HEINEMANN*
*Portsmouth, New Hampshire*
*London*

HEINEMANN EDUCATIONAL BOOKS, INC.
70 Court Street / Portsmouth, NH 03801
22 Bedford Square London WCIB 3HH
LONDON   EDINBURGH   MELBOURNE   AUCKLAND
SINGAPORE   NEW DELHI   IBADAN   NAIROBI
JOHANNESBURG   KINGSTON   PORT OF SPAIN

*Library of Congress Cataloging-in-Publication Data*
Smith, Frank, 1928–
   Joining the literacy club.

   Bibliography: p.
   Includes indexes.
   1. Literacy.   2. Learning.   3. Children—Language.
4. Educational sociology.   I.  Title.
LC149.S57   1988        370.19        87-25022
ISBN 0-435-08456-9
UK ISBN 0-435-10071-8

Designed by Wladislaw Finne.
Printed in the United States of America.

# Contents

*Cassette tapes of Frank Smith presenting the
eight talks on which the essays in this book
are based are available from ABEL PRESS,
P.O. Box 6162, Station C, Victoria, BC, Canada, V8P 5L5*

# Introduction

The essays in this collection pivot on a new metaphor for learning, reflected in the title of the first chapter and of the entire book. Learning, I propose, is primarily a social rather than an individual accomplishment. We learn from other people, not so much through conscious emulation as by "joining the club" of people we see ourselves as being like, and by being helped to engage in their activities. Usually we are not even aware that we are learning. One of the most important communities any individual can join is the "literacy club," because membership ensures that individuals learn how to read and write, and because reading is the entrance to many other clubs.

If there is a general theme that holds the essays together, it is that most significant people in every learner's life are teachers— the formal teachers of the classroom, the informal (and less frequently acknowledged) teachers in the world outside school, and the teachers (scarcely ever recognized) who are the authors of the books we read.

These essays were all written during the past three years, after I had released myself from my university commitments in Victoria. As an independent writer I have been able to travel more extensively and to meet a greater range of children, teachers, and researchers, exploring ideas on a wider variety of topics and submitting them to more intensive and productive argument. It is perhaps no coincidence that in the same period I have come to emphasize the social basis of learning.

The first essay in this book, "Joining the Literacy Club," examines the characteristics of the club that children must join if they are to become readers and writers, and the importance of the demonstrations and collaboration that teachers must provide if their students are to continue to learn. The second essay, "Reading Like a Writer," explores how apprentice readers and writers require the personal attention of their teachers for a short time only, until *authors*, the most experienced members of the literacy club, can take over. The third essay, "What's the Use of the Alphabet?," responds to a particular issue raised in the first two chapters.

The fourth essay, "Learning to Be a Critical Thinker," extends the theme of learning through club membership to something even more fundamental than reading, to thought itself, while "Collaboration in the Classroom" examines the dynamics of club situations in the frequently hostile environment of school. Computers will be a primary means by which club activities are developed or destroyed in classrooms, and their uses, good and bad, are discussed in the sixth essay, "The Promise and Threat of Computers in Language Education."

The final two essays focus on points of view. At the conclusion of my earlier collection of essays, *Essays into Literacy*, I proposed that it would be far more appropriate in education to regard the human brain as an artist, as a creator of worlds, than as a device for acquiring, storing, organizing and utilizing information. Literacy, I also argued, is more than the shunting of information between one person and another. It is the exploration of worlds of ideas and experience, for readers and writers alike. The penultimate essay in the present collection examines the nature and influence of educational metaphors more closely—including such ubiquitous terms as "process," "skills," "levels," and "stages."

A concluding metaphor, "How Education Backed the Wrong Horse," introduces an inquiry into a poor choice of theory. This choice led education away from the understanding that learning was a social activity and into the disastrous belief that effective and worthwhile learning could be rigorously controlled and individually delivered, one predetermined piece at a time.

My essays usually begin with ideas—my own and other people's—informally contemplated, discussed and argued, jotted down to see how they look in writing and to give them a chance to develop, presented in talks or workshops, and then further discussed, argued, elaborated, revised, and rewritten. Parts of the essays in turn find their way into my books, although I am never sure whether the ideas or examples in the books are generated spontaneously or come from reading, listening, lectures, arguments, essays, or long walks. Writing is not a compartmentalized activity.

Certain questions or comments almost predictably arise after I have publicly presented the thoughts in these essays, and I list a few of them in the "Postscripts" at the end of this book, together with my responses. I do not do this to claim the last word (which writers can never have), but to continue the discussion. The enormous advantage of language, as Karl Popper (1976) points out, is that it enables us to argue—not to persuade others but to test our own hypotheses. These essays are not intended to transmit information but to share explorations into language, learning, and education with other concerned members of the literacy club.

*Frank Smith*
Victoria, 1987

# Joining the literacy club

It is obvious that far more than formal instruction is involved when children learn how to read and write. No matter how systematic the instruction or how homogenized the material, children inevitably differ in how much they know and what they can demonstrate. This variation is frequently shrugged off as a matter of little interest. Of course children respond differently to instruction; they have had different out-of-school experiences. Such an observation is indisputable, but it raises more questions than it answers. What do children learn from those more general experiences in which there is no formal instruction? And what is the nature of those experiences? Why is informal experience so effective in children's learning?

Such questions are even more interesting to theorists and practitioners like me, who have not been persuaded that children learn to read and write as a consequence of formal instruction in any case. On the one hand there is no evidence that any child ever learned to read by simply being subjected to a program of systematic reading instruction (though unfortunately there is a good deal of evidence to the contrary). Theoretically there is no basis for believing that a child could become literate in such a way. The understanding that children need in order to become literate is just not available to them in reading drills and exercises (Smith, 1981a). On the other hand there is a growing mass of evidence that many children know a great deal about reading and writing even before they come to school, and have subtle and crucial insights about the nature of literacy itself (Goelman, Oberg and Smith, 1984).

These are all matters that require investigation. They are not entirely new or unique, however. Similar considerations apply to the vast amounts of learning about spoken language that very young children accomplish without the benefit of formal instruction. Very rapidly children learn to talk the way their family and friends talk. Even more rapidly they learn to understand the way other people speak. But children do not learn to talk like everyone they hear talking, even the ones they might hear talking most (like their schoolteachers, for example). What accounts for the differences? And how can children's success be explained?

My argument in this essay will be that children learn to read and write effectively only if they are admitted into a community of written language users, which I shall call the "literacy club," starting before the children are able to read or write a single word for themselves. Such a club has to be similar to the community of spoken language users to which infants are admitted almost from the moment of birth. The procedures are the same, and the benefits are the same—admission to the club rapidly results in becoming like established members in spoken language, in literacy, and in many other ways as well.

## The spoken language club

Infants join a spoken language club with a single unqualified reciprocal act of affiliation. There are no dues to be paid, no entry standards to be met, and there is no demand for references. A mutual acknowledgment of acceptance into the group is all that is required. Infants join the club of speakers that they take for granted they will be like; these are the kind of people the child is. The experienced members of the club in turn accept the child as one of them. They take for granted that the child will talk like them, and think and behave like them in every important way. Expectation does not guarantee learning, of course, but it makes it possible. Expectation that learning will *not* take place almost inevitably produces the contrary effect.

There is nothing special about the spoken language clubs to which everyone belongs. They function in much the same way as any special interest group. Members are concerned about each other's interests and welfare, and go out of their way to provide all manner of social events and other kinds of incidental benefits. In particular, members occupy themselves with whatever activities the club has formed itself to promote, constantly demonstrating the value and utility of these activities to the new members, helping them to participate when they want but never forcing their involvement and never ostracizing them for not having the understanding or the expertise of more practiced members. Differences in ability and in specific interests are taken for granted.

## THE BENEFITS OF MEMBERSHIP

Try to imagine the advantages for infants of acceptance into the spoken language club:

1. They see what spoken language does. As Halliday has pointed out, children do not learn language as an abstract system which they then apply to various uses; they learn language and its uses simultaneously (Halliday, 1973). The uses of language are complex and manifold: it can be used in support of every human endeavor, physical, cognitive, and emotional. But none of these uses is self-evident; all must be demonstrated to those who do not yet know. And the multiplicity of ways in which "people like them" use spoken language are continually demonstrated to children in the spoken language club they join.
2. Infants are admitted as junior members. No one in the club expects newcomers to talk or to understand like fully fledged members, but no one doubts that they will attain mature competence in due course. There is no discrimination, no attempt to exclude beginners from club activities. They are not labeled. Mistakes are expected, not frowned upon or punished as undesirable behavior.
3. People *help* infants to become experts. There is no formal instruction, no special time when they are expected to learn. Instead, someone helps them to say what they are trying to say and to understand what they are trying to understand. The help is always relevant, so that the learner never has to ask or wonder what it is for.
4. Infants are quickly admitted into a full range of club activities, as the activities make sense to them and are useful to them. New members are never required to be involved in some-

thing they do not understand. They are never engaged in activity that appears to be pointless. Everything that language can do for the other members of the club is revealed to them, in the expectation that they in turn will want to make use of language in the same ways.

5. Infants *learn* at a rate that remains phenomenal even to those who have studied it most. Their vocabulary grows at an average rate of over twenty words a day (Miller, 1977), and the grammar that enables them to understand and be understood by other members of the club develops rapidly to a complexity that confounds linguistic description. Children learn subtle and intricate rules of *cohesion*, of how sentences are organized into coherent statements and conversations, which are never explicitly taught and which most people do not realize they observe. Children learn many complex and crucial rules of *register* that enable us to say things appropriately according to where we are talking, whom we are talking to, and what we are talking about. Children learn thousands of idioms, which grammar and vocabulary do not make intelligible but which are the way language is actually used. They learn intonation, which is another multilayered set of complicated rules. They learn grammars of gesture, of eye contact, and of such delicate matters as how close one may stand to various people during conversation. How much children learn about language, unknown to themselves and to others, staggers the imagination and defies comprehensive research analysis.

6. One other matter children learn, which is perhaps more important to them than any I have mentioned. They learn that the language we speak identifies us as members of a particular group. Members of different clubs, of different communities, do not speak in the same way. Our own particular language is an emblem of all our cultural ties. Language is as personal and as significant as clothing, hairstyle, and ornamentation. To try to change a person's language is to reject the very essence of that person. We talk like the people we perceive ourselves to be. We resist efforts to make us talk like people we separate ourselves from, and we mistrust people who try to talk as if they are in our club when they are not.

JOINING OTHER CLUBS

Babies join other clubs, of course. Spoken language is far from all they learn during their first crowded years of life, strangers in a strange land, as they become more and more like those people—not necessarily the ones who gave birth to them—among whom they grow up. They join the clubs of people who walk as they will, dress as they will, do their hair and ornament themselves as they will, gesture as they will, eat the food they will, and who share common interests and feelings. They learn conventional ways of organizing the entire world, of dividing it into particular kinds of flowers and trees, horses and cows, knives and forks, categories, relationships, values and imperatives. They learn *culture*, the huge all-embracing clubs to which all of us belong. Always there is the same selectivity—we join the clubs of people whom we see as being like us, who see us as being like them. Always there is the same exclusiveness. We reject clubs if we do not see ourselves as belonging to them, and differentiate ourselves from others whom we do not accept as belonging to our clubs. If we do not want to belong to a particular club, or if we are deliberately excluded, then we learn not to be like the people in that club.

None of this learning stops with childhood. It continues throughout our adult lives, although it is so common, so inconspicuous, that we are usually unaware that it is taking place and may be reluctant even to call it learning when it is pointed out to us. We have become so persuaded that learning is difficult—from those occasions when, usually at someone else's behest, we have deliberately applied ourselves to a learning task—that we want to call it something else when we gain knowledge, understanding, or new behavior simply by virtue of our particular club memberships. Yet we read the newspaper or watch a television program, and the next day we can discuss the experience with a friend. We remember what we had for breakfast yesterday, what we wore to the picnic last week, what the newest things are in whatever our interests or pastimes happen to be. We may go to the movies and come out walking and talking like the particular character who attracted our attention, all without effort, usually quite unconsciously, and sometimes even against our will. All of this is learning, all of this is doing the things done by the kind of person we see ourselves as being, keeping up with the activities of the club.

Adults maintain their club memberships. The major difference with children is that they do everything from scratch. Perhaps that is the reason the bonds to all our childhood clubs seem so durable. Our strongest affiliations are to the clubs we join first.

Consider some advantages of membership in the clubs children first join, like the spoken language club of the people who speak the way they will speak. All of the learning takes place without risk. There are no formal tests, no examinations, no one expects all members to be as good as everyone else or to "progress" at the same rate. Help is often available and almost invariably relevant to what the learner is trying to do. Inability is met with understanding and assistance, not with a low grade and a kit of drills and exercises. Formal instruction may be frequently offered and even asked for, but it is always relevant to something the learner wants to know or do. It is always in the context of ongoing club activities. It makes sense. There are no planned schedules of learning, no curriculum committees, no accountability, no objectives, no prerequisites, and nothing is tested except in use.

LEARNING THROUGH CLUB MEMBERSHIP

There are seven important aspects or characteristics of the learning that takes place through membership in such clubs as the club of spoken language users. The learning is always (1) meaningful, (2) useful, (3) continual and effortless, (4) incidental, (5) collaborative, (6) vicarious, and (7) free of risk. These characteristics are worth considering in detail.

1. The learning is meaningful because it is always related to what the learner is doing, trying to do, or trying to understand. There is no need to have its relevance pointed out or taken on trust. The infant hears one club member saying "Pass the salt" and another passes the salt. The infant mutters "Wanna dwink" or even "Goo goo goo" and the more fluent member says "Please may I have a drink." Anything that is not meaningful is in fact ignored. A basic principle of children's learning seems to be "Don't pay attention to

what you don't understand." What is the point of trying to learn something that is meaningless? Instead, children—like sensible adults—devote their attention not to what they know already (which is boring) or to what they don't understand (which is confusing) but to what they do understand but don't already know (which is what anyone does who reads a newspaper).

2. A related basic principle of children's learning seems to be "Don't pay attention to anything that appears useless." Once again it is easy to see the adaptive value of such an attitude, even if it is (like the first principle) not frequently respected in school. I have already noted Halliday's important observation that children learn the uses of language as they learn language itself. In fact they learn language through its uses. Language is not learned by children for its potential, but for what it will do right now. The potential comes with having it. In the club of spoken language users, language is always used for a purpose. Club activities always have a point. By participating in club activities, children both see and learn through the uses of language.

3. Learning in the club is never an occasional or sporadic matter. If it were, the club would be boring and members wouldn't stay in very long. Instead, learning is continuous and effortless, so much so that we are usually unaware that it is taking place. Neither the learners nor the "teachers" are aware of the roles they are playing. Learning that is effortful is learning that is badly organized in some way, or not taking place at all.

4. Much of the spoken language children learn is learned incidentally rather than intentionally. Learning about language is not the primary aim, but rather the by-product of some other activity. I call this my "Can I have another donut?" theory of language learning. Every child learns to say "Can I have another donut?" not as a linguistic exercise, not as an expression of curiosity about language or even because of a biological predisposition to make meaningful sounds, but in order to get another donut. And in the course of getting another donut, as an incidental consequence, the child learns to say "Can I have another donut?" Language is learned for its uses *at the time*. As it is put to use, so it is learned.

5. Children recruit adults and other more experienced members of the spoken language club as unwitting collaborators. If they cannot say something they want to say, or cannot understand something they want to understand, they make an approximation, they do the best they can, and probably more often than not someone helps them out. Something relevant is made clear to them at the time it helps most by others who would rarely perceive themselves as collaborators, let alone as teachers, in what is essentially a child-controlled situation. The child employs more accomplished practitioners as resources, and neither party recognizes the productiveness and value of the mutual accomplishment. The social and collaborative basis of learning has been analyzed in great detail by Vygotsky (1978), who asserted that everything children can do with help one day, they can do by themselves another.

6. Children do more than use fellow members of their clubs as resources for providing the knowledge and understanding they need. They learn from what the others themselves do; the learning is *vicarious*. This is perhaps the most controversial assertion that I am making. Vicarious learning is not something that most experimental and cognitive psychologists have been particularly interested in for the past forty years, especially on the part of humans. Researchers have been far too busy analyzing what the learners themselves do. But the only way I can account for the enormous amounts of unwitting learning that children accomplish, much of it apparently error-free on the first trial, is that children actually learn from what other people do—*provided they are the kind of people the children see themselves as being*. Children do not rehearse very much; it is rare to find them practicing how they will talk (as opposed to actually making use of what they can say). Rather, children's competence seems to grow with a mature flower on every shoot. We might say that they "repeat" what they have heard someone else say, or that they "mimic" or "model" what someone else has done, but the behavior that is "copied" tends to be behavior that springs forth fully formed. Awkwardness and error are so rare in the way children demonstrate their advancing abilities—out of school at least—that we tend to regard the occasional anomaly as "cute." But then I think

again of the manner in which we all occasionally catch ourselves unwittingly talking or otherwise behaving like a person who has impressed us in some way, the kind of person
we see ourselves as being like, without any practice or rehearsal. Someone else has done something, and we have
learned.

7. I have little to add to the no-risk aspect of the learning that
   children are able to accomplish by virtue of being accepted
   into membership in the spoken language club, except that
   it may be its most important characteristic. How much risk
   of punishment, failure, or embarrassment would anyone run
   in order to learn in any club—before learning that the club
   itself might be hazardous?

## Joining the literacy club

Recent research in a number of cultures has shown that many
children know a great deal about reading and writing before
they get to school, or independently of what they are taught
in school (Goelman, Oberg and Smith, 1984). They know
many of the uses of written language, its role in signs, labels,
lists, letters, books, and television guides. They know what
people do with written language, even if they cannot do these
things themselves. They also know roughly how written language works, that it consists of letters written on lines, that it
is laid out in various conventional ways, and that there are rules
or regularities of spelling. They also have ideas about why
people read, even before they can read themselves. They pre-
tend to read and write in their role-playing games.

How do children learn all this? Not by programs or formal
instruction. There are no kits of materials and exercises for
teaching children how the world uses reading and writing.
They learn—usually without anyone being aware that they are
learning—by participating in literate activities with people who
know how and why to do these things. They join the literacy
club. People write with them and read with them—lists, notes,
letters, signs, directions, recipes—any of the routine "literacy
events" of daily life in which the child can share. Sometimes
the child seeks help, instruction even, to achieve something
that meets the child's specific purposes. But sometimes the
assistance is completely casual, as when someone points out

that an approaching sign says "Stop" or "Burgers" just as one might say to a child, "Look, there's a horse!"

Membership in the literacy club offers identical advantages to a child as membership in the spoken language and other clubs. Children see what written language is for, all of its manifold utilities for writers and for readers. They are admitted as junior members; no one expects them to be very skilled themselves, but they are helped to write and read whenever they have a purpose or interest of their own in such activities. Children get involved in an ever-broadening range of literate activities as these make sense to them, and the learning follows. Why should children join such a club even before they know a thing about reading and writing themselves? Children do so because they can see others engaging profitably in literacy activities who are the kind of people the children see themselves as being. Admission is once again a mutual act of acceptance. There is no exclusion.

There are unique advantages to joining the literacy club. Children can recruit as unwitting collaborators individuals who are not actually present, who might even be dead. Children can learn literacy from the authors they read. In *Writing and the Writer* (Smith, 1982b), I analyzed the enormous amount of knowledge that a writer of just average competence and experience accumulates about spelling, punctuation, capitalization, paragraphing, layout, grammar, style, genre, register, and other intricate and specialized aspects of written language. The only source available for all that knowledge is not instruction but what other people have written. Authors, in other words, teach us how to write what we would like to write. They are our collaborators as we learn to write ourselves. At the Institute for Education at the University of London, Margaret Spencer (1987) has argued that the authors of children's stories teach children how to read. The children follow a familiar or predictable tale, perhaps with adult assistance, and the author shows how the story is actually told in written language. In other words, the greatest help to newcomers in the club of readers and writers may be those most experienced members who never tire of being approached and interrogated, the authors of the printed page.

The experience available to even the youngest children in the literacy club has the same crucial seven characteristics for learning that I discussed for the club of spoken language users. New members are assimilated into a world where written language is (1) meaningful—people pay attention to signs and labels and books because they make sense. The activities are also (2) useful—all the reading and writing that is done is done for a purpose. The learning is (3) continual and effortless—every encounter with print is an opportunity to add something to one's repertoire of useful knowledge. Much of the learning is also (4) incidental—practically every child in the world learns to recognize the word *McDonald's*, not in order to be able to recognize the word itself, but as a by-product of getting a hamburger. Learning in the literacy club is almost invariably (5) collaborative as other people, at your side or on the page, help you to understand what you want to understand or to express what you want to express. Such learning, I again believe, is frequently (6) vicarious—the author writes something and the reader learns. I call reading in this way *reading like a writer*. As I explain in the following essay, we can read as if we were writing what we read—and in effect the author writes for us. And finally, such learning opportunities in the literacy club are (7) no-risk. A child striving to read or write something is helped and encouraged, not given a low grade and a program of exercises. Members of the literacy club are people who read and write, even the beginners, and the fact that one is not very competent yet is no reason for exclusion or ridicule. A newcomer is the same kind of person as the most proficient club member, except that he or she hasn't yet had as much experience. It is the same in all normal sports and recreational clubs.

## Teachers and schools

The role of teachers in all of this is very clear. Teachers should facilitate and promote the admission of children into the literacy club. Children who come to school already members of the club, who regard themselves as the kind of people who read and write, should find expanded opportunities in school for engaging in all the activities of club membership. Children who have not become members before they get to school should find the classroom the place where they are immediately admitted to the club. The classroom should be a place full of meaningful and useful reading and writing activities, where participation is possible without evaluation and collaboration is always available. No child should be excluded.

This means, of course, that every reading and writing teacher should be a member of the club. Many teachers are surprised when they reflect upon what they actually demonstrate to children about reading and writing during the school day. How many teachers are seen reading a novel or a magazine for pleasure? How many are seen writing a letter, a poem, or a story? What might children assume reading and writing to be from the kinds of written language activity they see teachers engaging in? Is it surprising that many children, and not only the least able, think reading and writing are "work," punitive, boring, and essentially useless school rituals?

Not that the teacher need be the sole collaborator. Many people can help children to read and write themselves. Other children in the class, children from other classrooms, other adults, visitors, and guests can all collaborate. Any member of the literacy club can help children become readers and writers. The teacher's role is to ensure that the club exists and that every child is in it.

THE CONSTRAINTS OF PROGRAMS

Of course, most schools are nothing like this. Many teachers cannot imagine a classroom without evaluation, although tests never taught a child anything (except perhaps that he or she is not a member of the club). The clubs in the world outside school never grade, never give scores or marks. It is taken for granted that junior members will attempt things beyond their capacity, but it is also taken for granted that they will learn in due course, and no one sees any point in keeping a record of passing inadequacies. Many teachers cannot imagine a classroom without drills and exercises, the "activities" that are supposed to teach children reading and writing but which so often persuade them that reading and writing are nonsensical activities.

I have written elsewhere about the nature of reading and writing *programs*, a term I use for any endeavor by someone outside the classroom to determine systematically and in advance what teachers and learners should do next in the classroom (Smith, 1981b). Such programs rarely engage children in meaningful reading and writing activities (except in the mind of the program developer). The language of their exercises is purposeless—fragmented, decontextualized, and trivial. If anything, they teach that written language is artificial. The developers and promoters of such programs entertain the awesome belief that literacy can be taught to a child one predetermined skill at a time, and that a child who masters every exercise to a criterion level will eventually become a reader and a writer. This is the antithesis of the literacy club. Consider for a final time the seven characteristics of learning situations.

None of the drills, exercises, and tests of formal programmatic instruction demonstrate that writing is (1) meaningful or (2) useful. Their only purpose is their own instructional ends. The only evident reason for a child to do the task is to get it over with, to get the mark, or because the teacher says so. It would be a joke to suggest that such learning is (3) continual and effortless—it is sporadic, laborious, and often stressful. The learning is never (4) incidental—you learn what is there to be learned because it is your assignment. The only thing that might be learned incidentally, beyond the intent of the program developer, is, unhappily, that reading and writing are meaningless, laborious, and often stressful.

The learning is also rarely (5) collaborative—it is usually taken for granted that each child works for himself or herself, and cooperation is regarded as a dilution of effort, if not as cheating. (I have discovered that students of all ages, from primary school to graduate school, are reluctant to collaborate on assignments, even when required to do so. They fear they will lose something. In what kind of club do students learn that collaboration is an undesirable activity?) Programmatic learning cannot be (6) vicarious—children working their way through exercises and activities rarely see a more proficient person doing what they are supposed to be learning, certainly not in any meaningful sense. And as for being (7) no-risk, systematic instruction is the very contrary. Every step along the way the concern is "to get it right," to get a good grade. To fall behind is to risk the most damaging of labels. If you don't perform well enough on the rituals, you may not ever get the opportunity actually to read and write.

Why then do we have so many programs in schools? Why do school systems buy them (which is the reason publishers produce them)? This again is a complex issue, dealt with at length in *Insult to Intelligence* (Smith, 1986), but I can outline a few reasons here. The first is that schools are strange institutions; one might almost argue that they are organized to prevent the formation of clubs. Schools wall themselves off from the world outside. They barricade children into large cells in which everybody is roughly expected to do the same thing at the same time at the same rate. Children are segregated according to age and ability as if the ideal were that no one should be able to help anyone else. Halls, which elsewhere are supposed to facilitate communication, are expected to be kept empty except at specified times.

A second reason for the pervasiveness of programs in education is inertia. Systematized instruction has been around for so long that many people cannot imagine education without it. When programs are found wanting (as they inevitably are —no one would claim that students as a group read or write any better now than they did twenty years ago, when programmatic instruction first began to proliferate), the solution is always to impose more and "better" programs. Schools of education train new teachers to be dependent upon programs, and when professors are asked why they do this (when many of them know programs do not produce readers and writers), they say it is what schools want, it is what schools are like.

A third reason for the spread of programmatic instruction is an egregious error in research and practice—the notion that if you analyze in detail everything an expert can do and teach these things one at a time to a beginner, then the beginner will become an expert. Experts know the alphabet, so we'll teach the alphabet. Experts can do phonics, so we'll insist upon phonics. Experts are good spellers (possibly) so we'll demand perfect spelling. All of this overlooks how and why experts acquire all these skills in the first place and ends up getting everything backwards. Reading makes you good at phonics, rather than phonics making you good at reading. Membership in the club makes all the skills available to you, but the demands for separate skills as prerequisites simply keep you out of the club.

But the final, most potent and destructive reason for all of the programs we have is *control*—a matter of power and trust. Teachers need programs if they do not trust children to learn, if they feel they must control their learning every step of the way. And people outside the classroom insist on programs if they do not trust teachers to teach, if they feel they must control what teachers do every step of the way. The issue is not pedagogical at all—it is political.

## THE TEACHER'S RESPONSIBILITY

As I have said, the prime responsibility for any teacher concerned with literacy must be to ensure that clubs exist and that no child is excluded from them. In simple terms, this means lots of collaborative and meaningful reading and writing activities, the kinds of things that are often characterized as extras, rewards or even "frills," things like stories (reading and writing), poems, plays, letters, newspapers, magazines, posters, menus, notes, packages, reviews. . . . There would not be enough time in the day for all of the possibilities even if there were no programs.

Anything a child is not interested in doing should be modified or avoided. Forcing a child into boring or painful activity will merely teach the child that the activity is boring or painful, no matter how good we think it is for the child. Anything with a mark attached should be avoided. Children quickly learn that many school activities are worth doing only for the grade, and when they learn that, they learn that the activity is intrinsically worthless. And anything a child does not want to know at this moment might just as well be set aside—which means that most "correction" is pointless. The general consequences of jumping on children's reading and writing errors is that they read and write less, and therefore learn less. Correction is worthwhile only when children demand it themselves, which they will do only if they see themselves as members of the club, when they expect and require to become fully competent participants in their own right.

Of course, teachers should try to eliminate programs as much as they can, but I must acknowledge that this is often difficult if not impossible for the simple reason that programs are imposed or urged upon them by outside authorities who may be well-meaning but who do not understand children or language. Many quite sincerely believe that the only way to ensure sound education is to control totally what teachers do, and they are not aware of the cost of this view. That is why teachers must educate their administrators and the general public, especially politicians and parents.

But the course that all teachers can adopt immediately to protect themselves and students from programmatic excesses is to recognize the difference between literacy "instruction" and meaningful reading and writing activities, and to be honest about these differences with their students. The danger is not so much that students are required to engage in futile tests and exercises as the fact that they (and their parents) quickly come to believe that the tests and exercises are important. Students and parents—and even some teachers—think that the tests and exercises *are* reading and writing. The children do not even understand the club which they are supposed to have joined.

An ideal educational system is not required before all children can be introduced into the literacy club. Certainly more might be done educationally and politically to recognize the importance of the club and the futility of programmatic instruction. But even given schools as they are, there should always be room for teachers to expand the activities of literacy clubs, in which all children have an opportunity to engage with more experienced members in productive and rewarding reading and writing activities, in classrooms and outside. The overriding concern must always be that no child is excluded.

# Reading like a writer

**2** The first time I explored in detail how children learn to write, I was tempted to conclude that it was, like the flight of bumblebees, a theoretical impossibility. I dissected the trivializing oversimplification that writing is basically a matter of handwriting and a few spelling and punctuation rules. I questioned the myth that one could learn to write by diligent attention to instruction and practice. And I was left with the shattering conundrum that writing requires an enormous fund of specialized knowledge that cannot possibly be acquired from lectures, textbooks, drill, trial and error, or even from the exercise of writing itself. A teacher may set tasks for children that result in the production of a small but acceptable range of sentences, but much more is required to become a competent and adaptable author of letters, reports, memoranda, journals, term papers, and perhaps occasional poems or pieces of fiction appropriate to the demands and opportunities of out-of-school situations.

Where do people who write acquire all the knowledge they need? The conclusion I reached was as puzzling as the riddles it was supposed to resolve, because I decided that it could only be through reading that writers learn all the intangibles they know. And not only is there an unfortunate abundance of evidence that people who read do not necessarily become competent writers, but I had myself argued that fluent readers need not pay attention to matters like spelling and punctuation. To learn to write, children must read in a special kind of way.

This essay will follow the course of my reasoning. First, I shall show that writing demands far more specialized knowledge than is usually realized, very little of which can be contained within formal instruction. Next, I shall argue why this knowledge can only be acquired from a particular kind of reading. I shall then illustrate how this kind or reading occurs and show that children are very experienced at learning in this way. Finally, I shall consider how teachers can facilitate such learning.

## The complexity of writing

Even the most ordinary kinds of text involve a vast number of conventions that could never be organized into formal instructional programs. The scope and scale of such conventions are generally unsuspected by teachers and learners alike. Spelling, for example, demands the memorization of every word we are ever likely to write. The "rules" of spelling can be numbered in the hundreds and still carry only a fifty percent probability of being correct for any particular word. There are so many alternatives and exceptions that we must confirm and memorize the correct spelling of every word we hope to write with confidence in the future, even if it does happen to be "regular." When does anyone check the spelling of all the words that are routinely spelled correctly, let alone commit them to memory?

Punctuation, capitalization and other "rules" of grammar are essentially circular and meaningless to anyone who cannot already do what is being "explained." Children are instructed to begin sentences with a capital letter and to end them with a period, but if they ask what a sentence is they will sooner or later be told that it is something that begins with a capital letter and ends with a period. The statement that a sentence is a "complete thought" is as inaccurate and useless as the assertion that a word is a "unit of meaning" or that a paragraph is organized around a single main idea. How would anyone recognize in isolation a unit of meaning, a complete thought, or a main idea? Linguists are unable to make any constructive use of such statements, which are definitions, not rules of application. They are meaningless to anyone without an implicit understanding of the conventions that determine what shall constitute a word, sentence, or paragraph, conventions that differ from one language to another. Unfortunately, those in possession of such implicit understanding tend to find the definitions transparently obvious and to regard them as the basis of learning rather than the consequence of having learned. Obviously anyone who can write must have knowledge of these conventions, but it is not the kind of knowledge that can be made explicit and taught to others.

Even arbitrary rules, descriptions, and definitions evade us when it comes to such subtle matters as *style*, the intricate *registers* that depend upon the topic of discussion and the audience addressed, and the *schemas* appropriate to the particular medium being employed. Not only must letters, telegrams, formal and informal notes, newspaper reports, magazine articles, short stories, and poems be composed differently, the format of each genre itself varies depending on its specific purpose. Letters to close friends and to the bank manager have no more in common than news items in the *National Enquirer* and the *Wall Street Journal*. These conventions remain to be fully investigated by linguists, who have only recently begun to analyze many critical aspects of language that everyone observes and expects, in speech and in competent writing, without awareness of their existence. There are, for example, the complex rules of *cohesion*, which link sentences together and to the nonlanguage context. As Halliday and Hasan (1976) pointed out in their pioneering analysis of this intricate system, cohesion puts the texture into text. How could any of this be reduced to a few prescriptions, formulas, or drills? Even if we could and do learn a few hundred spellings, some useful grammatical constructions, and some precepts of punctuation through diligent study at school, these would be only a fraction of the expertise an average journeyman writer requires.

What about learning by trial and error, or "hypothesis testing"? I thought the answer must be that we learn to write by writing until I reflected upon how little anyone writes at school, even the eager students, and how little feedback is provided. Errors may be pointed out, but how often are relevant correct models provided, especially beyond the level of words? How often is such feedback studied attentively and acted upon, especially by those who need correction most? No one writes enough to learn more than a small fraction of what writers need to know. Most experienced writers can produce text that is right the first time, or at least they can edit or rewrite their more hurried drafts into conventional form, without extensive feedback. Besides, if we learn to write by having our hypotheses tested, where do these hypotheses come from? Practice and feedback may contribute toward polishing writing skills but cannot account for their acquisition in the first place (Krashen, 1984).

Learners need to find and assimilate a multitude of facts and examples, ranging from individual spellings to the appropriate organization of complex texts. Where can all these facts and examples be found, when they are not available in the lectures, textbooks, and exercises to which children are exposed in classrooms? The only possible answer seemed as obvious to me as I hope it now is to the reader—they must be found in what other people have written, in existing texts. To learn how to write for newspapers you must read newspapers; textbooks about newspapers will not suffice. For magazines, browse through magazines rather than through correspondence courses on magazine writing. To write poetry, read it. For the typical style of memoranda that circulate in your school, consult the school files.

All this became self-evident once I had dispelled my own illusion that prescriptive instruction might be able to convey even a modicum of what writers need to know. Written language in use displays all of its own relevant conventions. It demonstrates its own appropriate grammar, punctuation, and manifold stylistic devices, and it is a showcase for the spelling of words. So now I knew where the knowledge that writers require resides—in existing texts, ready for the reading, on the printed page. The question becomes the enigma of how such expanses of knowledge get into the heads of readers so that they become writers themselves.

The answer cannot be that all this specialized knowledge is learned by rote through innumerable deliberate formal analyses, by sitting down with texts and making extensive notes, or submitting endless data and examples to memory. What is learned is too complicated and subtle, and there is too much of it. There is not enough time. Instead it must be that the learning takes place without deliberate effort, even without awareness. We learn to write without suspecting that we are learning or what we learn. Everything points to the necessity of learning to write from what we read, as we read. That is the trick to be explained.

## Learning as a collaborative activity

The alternative I propose is that knowledge of all the conventions of writing gets into our head like much of our knowledge of spoken language, and indeed of the world in general, without awareness that learning is taking place. The learning is unconscious, effortless, incidental, vicarious, and essentially collaborative. It is incidental because we learn when learning is not our primary intention, vicarious because we learn from what someone else does, and collaborative because we learn through others who help us to achieve our own ends.

Consider the range and extent of the spoken language that children learn during the first four or five years of their lives. Miller (1977) estimated that infants add words to their vocabulary at an average rate of one every hour they are awake, a total of several thousand a year. Young children learn grammar (in order to talk and to be understood) with a complexity that defies linguistic analysis. They master a multitude of idiomatic expressions and intricate nuances of cohesion and register most adults do not suspect they themselves observe, let alone their children. They learn complex subtleties of intonation and gesture. They do all this without formal instruction, with very little evident trial and error, and with no deliberate diagnostic or remedial intervention at all.

There is an exquisite selectivity. Children first begin talking like their parents, then like their peers, and later, perhaps, like their favorite entertainment or sporting personalities. They do not learn to talk like everyone they hear speaking, even those they may hear most. They learn the language of the groups to which they belong (or expect to belong) and resist the language of the groups they reject or from which they are rejected. They learn—as I have said in the previous essay—from the clubs to which they belong.

This pervasive learning extends far beyond the structures and customs of language to mannerisms, dress, ornamentation, and other significant patterns of behavior. It takes place in the absence of overt motivation or deliberate intention (as many of us know who have come away from a film or a book acting the part of one of the characters). *Engagement* is the term I have used to describe such learning (Smith, 1981a). It is not learning that takes place as a consequence of what someone else does, but rather learning that occurs concurrently with the other person's act—provided it is our act too. The other person's behavior is our own learning trial. We learn when the other person does something we would like to do and take for granted we shall be able to do.

Adults have neither the time nor the expertise to teach spoken language to children. Instead they act as a source of information for children and as unwitting collaborators. They are overheard as they talk to each other, and thereby show children why and how speech can be used. They demonstrate spoken language being used for purposes that children will come to expect to accomplish themselves. Often the explanation of the language is embedded in the situation in which it is used—someone says "Pass the salt" and the salt is passed. Television is replete with such examples, especially in commercial announcements. Sometimes the explanation is explicit, as adults or peers elaborate upon a meaning for a child, though the intention is usually no more deliberately pedagogical than when a child is told "Look, there's a McDonald's." And if a child wants to say something, an adult or more competent friend helps the child to say it. No one gives a child struggling to be understood a low grade and a kit of instructions. But children do not need to be personally involved to learn to say what they would like to be able to say. They learn when they hear others talk for a purpose they understand, which they take for granted they can share. In effect, adults and peers admit children into the club of people who talk as they do. They do not expect children to be experts in advance, nor do they anticipate failure. There are no prerequisites for admission.

In such circumstances, children learn from what they overhear by "listening like a talker." They do not regard the language from which they learn as anything remote, an attribute of others, but rather as something they themselves would want and expect to do. The children become "spontaneous apprentices," as Miller (1977) felicitously puts it, engaging in the enterprises of adults or peers who act as their unsuspecting surrogates in the trial and error of learning. And since the surrogates are experienced they tend to have a variety of trials and very few errors, a most efficacious combination if useful learning is to take place. The only source of the complex and subtle spoken language children learn for their own social groups must be the speech they hear in those groups, to which they can listen like a talker. And clearly, all children who can talk like their family and friends must be very good at listening and learning in that way. They must have been doing it from before the time they could say a word for themselves.

Obviously children do not learn about spoken language from everything they hear spoken. Sometimes they do not understand and sometimes they are not interested, two situations which all teachers know are not conducive to learning (except to learning that something is confusing and boring). Obviously also, children (and adults) can attend to and understand what is said without talking like a particular speaker. We frequently "listen like a listener," when we attend to what is said but have no desire or expectation that we should come away talking like the speaker. We do not see ourselves as belonging to that particular club. We are not that kind of person, and the vicarious engagement does not take place. The consequence of not being a member of the club is dramatic, for children and for adults. We do not learn. In effect, the brain learns not to learn; it shuts down its own sensitivity (Smith, 1981a). Exclusion from any club of learners is a condition difficult to reverse, whether we impose it upon ourselves or have it imposed upon us.

## Collaboration with authors

I have discussed how adults and more competent peers act as unwitting collaborators so that children can learn about spoken language. Children learn vicariously, provided they can "listen like a talker" by virtue of their implicit membership in the particular club to which the practitioners they hear speaking belong. My argument now is that everyone who becomes a competent writer uses authors in exactly the same way, even children who may not yet be able to write a word. They must read like a writer in order to learn how to write like a writer. There is no other way in which the intricate complexity of a writer's knowledge can be acquired.

Most literate adults are familiar with the experience of pausing unexpectedly while reading a newspaper, magazine, or book, and then going back to look at the spelling of a word that has caught their attention. We say to ourselves "Ah, so that's how that word is spelled," especially if the word is a familiar one that we have previously only heard, like a name on radio or television. The word may or may not be spelled the way we would expect it to be spelled. It just looks new. We did not begin reading in order to have a spelling lesson, and we are not aware of paying attention to spelling (and to every other technical aspect of the writing) as we read. But we notice the unfamiliar spelling—in the same way that we would notice an incorrect one—because we are writing the text as we read it. We are reading like a writer, or at least like a speller. We notice the words whose spelling we ought to know, that we expect to know, because we are the kind of person who knows about spelling.

Here is a second example. Once more we are casually reading, and once more we find ourselves pausing to reread a passage, not because of the spelling this time or because we did not understand the passage. In fact we understood it very well. We go back because something in the passage was particularly well put, because we respond to the craftsman's touch. We have read something we would like to be able to write ourselves but also something we think is not beyond our reach. We have been reading like a writer, like a member of the club.

On neither of these two occasions would I want to say that we learn as a consequence of what we read. We do not turn aside from our reading to study the spelling or the stylistic device we have noticed. If we learn at all, we learn at the single encounter, vicariously, concurrently. If we can write at all we must have learned much more than we realize. In fact I am inclined to think that the new spelling, like the well-turned phrase, attracts our adult attention because it is an exception, because we already know the spellings of most of the words we read. We must have been adding to our repertoire of spellings at a rate approaching that at which children learn spoken words, that is hundreds if not thousands a year. We were no more aware of the occasions on which we learned specific aspects of writing than we were conscious of learning the meaning of all the words we know. It is only after the event that we sometimes realize we have learned vicariously, when we find ourselves using the words, phrases, and stylistic idiosyncracies of a particular author we have been reading.

I do not want to say that even accomplished writers read like a writer *every* time they read. It does not happen when our attention is overloaded or when we have trouble trying to understand what we are reading. (How can one read like the writer of something one cannot understand?) There is not much opportunity to read like a writer when we are totally concerned with the act of reading, with getting every word right, or with trying to memorize all the facts. It does not happen when we have no interest in writing what we read. We do not come away talking like a telephone directory after looking up a few numbers. And there is no reading like a writer when we have no expectation of writing the kind of written language we read. The latter illustrates my essential point again, that learning occurs only when we perceive ourselves as members of the club. We can and often do read simply like a reader, for whatever purpose we are reading. But to learn to write we must read like a writer. Reading in this way need not affect comprehension. In fact it will promote comprehension because it is based upon prediction.

To read like a writer we engage vicariously with what the author is writing. We anticipate what the author will say, so that the author is in effect writing on our behalf, not simply showing how something is done but doing it with us. The situation is identical to that in spoken language when adults help children to say what they want to say or would like and expect to be able to say. The author becomes an unwitting collaborator. Everything the learner would want to spell the author spells. Everything the learner would want to punctuate the author punctuates. Every nuance of expression, every relevant syntactic device, every turn of phrase, the author and learner write together. Bit by bit, one thing at a time but incalculably often over the passage of time, the learner learns through *reading* like a writer to *write* like a writer.

Of course, these is also a need to write, especially for beginners. Writing enables one to perceive oneself as a writer, as a member of the club, and thus to learn to write by reading.

There is also a need for a teacher or other practitioner to be an immediate collaborator with the learning writer, for support and encouragement but also to provide knowledge of technicalities that a text cannot offer. Such technicalities range from the use of paper clips, index cards, and wastepaper baskets to the nature and utility of drafts and of editing, none of which is apparent in published texts and none of which, therefore, the author can demonstrate. One might add to the preceding list all the emotional concomitants of writing, from frustration to exhilaration, which people who are not experienced members of the writing club rarely seem to appreciate and which are frequently not dominant considerations in classrooms.

## The teacher's role

Teachers have two critically important functions in guiding children toward literacy. They must demonstrate uses for writing, and they must help children use writing themselves. Put in other words, teachers must show the advantages that membership in the club of writers offers and ensure that children can join.

Teachers do not have to *teach* children to read like writers, though they may indeed for a while have to see that beginners get help to read. And of course, teachers must help children to write—not teach them about writing—so that they can perceive themselves as members of the club of writers. Teachers must also ensure that children have access to reading materials that are relevant to the kind of writer they are interested in becoming at a particular moment. Teachers must recruit the authors who will become the children's unwitting collaborators.

Most importantly, teachers must help children to perceive themselves as readers and writers before the children are able to read and write for themselves.

It is not difficult to imagine how children can be helped to read before they can read for themselves. Someone else must do the reading for them. There is no need to fear that a child who is read to will become dependent or lazy. Children able to read something they want to read will not have the patience to wait for someone else to read for them, any more than they will wait for someone to say something on their behalf if they can say it for themselves.

It is instructive to observe what happens as young children are read to. First they allow someone else to read *to* them (they listen like a listener). Then the other person reads *with* them (they listen like a reader). Finally that most aggravating situation inevitably arises when the child wants to turn the page before the collaborator gets to the end of it (the child is reading). Of course, a teacher may not always have time to read with an individual child, but it is not necessary for the teacher always to do this personally. Other children may take the collaborative role, or children can be encouraged to read collaboratively in groups, or readers from outside the classroom can be recruited. The essential thing is for the reading to be a natural activity, preferably initiated by the child for the child's purposes, whether that purpose is to enjoy a story, to share a letter or a newspaper item, or to find out what is on the lunch menu or the television schedule for the day.

It may not be so easy to imagine how children can be helped to see themselves as authors before they are able to write. For a teacher (or some other collaborator) to act as a secretary for the child, taking care of the handwriting, spelling, punctuation and so forth, is not enough. There are many other decisions and conventions with which a beginner needs help, as the following example will illustrate.

The aim must be a collaboration so close that a child feels personally responsible for every word in a story (or poem or letter), even though the child might not have thought of a single word in the first place. First the child and the teacher have to establish that the child will write a story, that the child is to be an author. Then something like the following dialogue might ensue:

*Teacher:* What do you want to write a story about?
*Child:* I don't know. (The child's problem is identical to that of a university student confronted with selecting a dissertation topic: it is not that there is nothing to be written about, but that the number of alternatives is overwhelming.)
*Teacher:* (drawing on knowledge of the child's interests): Do you want to write about an astronaut, an alligator, a wicked witch, a baseball star, or yourself?
*Child:* An astronaut.
*Teacher:* (writes down the title): How does the story begin?
*Child:* I don't know.

The teacher offers some alternatives, the child selects, the teacher writes.

*Teacher:* What happens next?
*Child:* I don't know.

And so on. . . . Always the teacher offers alternatives from a range that will appeal to the child, and the child selects. This is especially important at the end. There is a myth that children (and many university students) can produce only very short texts. But with just the slightest encouragement they can in fact write on and on and on, until in principle I suppose the entire contents of their heads could be unraveled. The child's problem (and that of the university student) is most likely to be lack of knowledge of an appropriate convention for ending. There are standard ways to conclude any piece or writing; and if you do not know how to stop you might just as well stop now. So the teacher must offer a choice of exits.

And when they are done the child feels responsible for the entire story, as indeed the child was. This was a collaboration. The story would not have been written without the contribution of both parties. It makes no more sense to talk about who wrote what than to ask who carried which part if teacher and child move a table together that neither could move alone.

To become writers children must read like writers. And to read like writers they must perceive themselves as writers. Children—like adults—will read stories, poems, and letters differently when they see these texts as things they themselves could produce; they will write vicariously with the author. But to see themselves as writers they need collaboration with others who are more experienced members of the club.

There is no way of helping children to see themselves as writers if they are not interested. That is why the first responsibility of teachers must be to demonstrate to children that writing is interesting, possible, satisfying, and worthwhile. But there is also no way of helping children to become writers if the teacher does not believe that writing is interesting, possible, satisfying, and worthwhile. Teachers who are not themselves members of the club cannot admit children to it.

How can such teachers learn to see themselves as writers? They must read like writers themselves, and to do that they must, like children, collaborate with others who are willingly engaged in the enterprise of writing. For most teachers this should be easy—they can write with their own students in a collaboration so close that no one can say to whom the successes and the failures belong. What matters in the long run is not how expertly teachers or children may write, or whether they write separately or together, but the manner in which they will read when they regard themselves as members of the writers' club. Teachers who write poetry with children will find themselves reading poetry differently. They will be reading like members of the club of poets. And as members of the club, they will learn.

OVERCOMING THE HANDICAPS OF SCHOOL

Unfortunately schools may not be places in which children easily see themselves as members of the club of writers. Admission requirements and membership dues may be beyond many of them. The way in which schools are organized does not always encourage collaboration; it may favor instruction over demonstration and evaluation over purposeful activity. A "programmed" approach can reduce literacy to ritual and triviality for children, and leave little time for engagement with meaningful written language. Teachers can never be collaborators with children who regard them as taskmasters and antagonists.

The pervasiveness of the drill, exercises, tests, and rote learning of programmatic literacy activities is such that some teachers tend to lose touch with what written language is really for. I can offer a short and incomplete list that will encompass more meaningful reading and writing than is possible in any school day.

Written language is for stories to be read, books to be published, poems to be recited, plays to be acted, songs to be sung, newspapers to be circulated, letters to be mailed, jokes to be told, notes to be passed, cards to be sent, cartons to be labeled, instructions to be followed, designs to be made, recipes to be cooked, messages to be exchanged, programs to be organized, excursions to be planned, catalogs to be compared, entertainment guides to be consulted, memos to be distributed, announcements to be posted, bills to be collected, posters to be displayed, cribs to be hidden, and diaries to be concealed. Written language is for ideas, action, reflection and experience. It is not for having your ignorance exposed, your sensitivity bruised, or your ability assessed.

So how can teachers help children see the advantages and possibilities of the club of writers, despite all the constraints of school? Teachers must engage children in purposeful written language enterprises as often as possible and protect them from the destructive effect of meaningless activities that cannot otherwise be avoided. The first step is for teachers themselves to learn to distinguish meaningful writing from senseless ritual, and the second is to be open about the difference with children, to discuss it with them.

In particular, teachers should protect themselves and children from the disabling consequences of evaluation. Where evaluation and grading are unavoidable, as they so often are, it can be made clear to children that the "mark" is given for administrative or bureaucratic purposes that have nothing to do with "real world" writing. Grading never taught a writer anything (except that he or she was not a member of the club). Writers learn by learning about writing, not by getting letters or numbers put on their efforts and abilities. Children (and university students) who will write only for a grade have learned an odd notion of the advantages of the club of writers.

This is not a question of "correction," which in any case does not make anyone a better writer. Correction merely highlights what learners almost certainly know they cannot do in the first place. Correction is worthwhile only if the learner would seek it in any case, and to seek correction you must regard yourself as a professional, an established member of the club. I am not saying there should not be standards, but that the standards have to come from what the learner wants and expects to achieve. Emphasis on the suppression of errors results in the suppression of writing.

It is difficult for many teachers not to see evaluation as a necessity. Marks and grades probably pervade the very atmosphere in which they work and study. Teachers may not have been told of the devastating effect of such evaluation on sensitivity or of its inevitable connection with meaningless activities. Writing done for a purpose requires and permits no evaluation beyond fitness for that purpose, which can only be assessed by the learner through comparison with how the same purpose is achieved by more experienced members of the club. But that is the way children learn. They need not be directed to seek the best way of doing what they want to do: they look for it themselves. Children are never satisfied to speak an inadequate version of the language of the groups to which they adhere, any more than they want to dress or to ornament themselves in a less than conventional way. If they are members of a club, they want to conform to its standards. A child who does not want to learn is clearly demonstrating exclusion from the group, voluntary or imposed.

School should be the place where children are initiated into the club of writers as soon as possible, with full rights and privileges even as apprentices. They will read like writers and take advantage of everything the club offers if they are not denied admission at the threshold.

## Notes

An earlier version of this article was published in *Language Arts*, 1983, *60*, 5, 558–67.

The arguments beginning on page 18 concerning the inadequacy of "mechanics," which are the grist of programmatic writing instruction, are condensed from chapter 10 of *Writing and the Writer* (Smith, 1982b).

# What's the use of the alphabet?

**3** The soldiers of literacy, as the writer Kazantzakis called the letters of the alphabet, are the most conspicuous part of the written languages in which they are employed. They may also be the most misunderstood. The letters are often the first aspect of reading and writing taught to children, possibly with good reason, though not necessarily for the reason we think. The letters and their tenuous relationships to the sounds of speech become the source of enormous complication in reading and writing instruction through the emphasis on phonics on the one hand and on spelling on the other. The significance of the correspondences between letters and sounds is frequently exaggerated, and important connections between letters and the meaning of words are generally ignored.

In this essay, I shall first discuss the relationship of letters to sounds and to meaning, and then consider the relevance of these relationships to reading and writing and to learning to read and write. Finally I shall examine some substantial but less familiar advantages of the alphabet, which facilitate literacy and a good deal more.

## The alphabet, sounds, and meaning

The word *alphabet* tells us nothing about what the alphabet does. It is merely the juxtaposed names of the first two letters of the Greek alphabet, alpha and beta, as if we were to call our number system the one-two. The Greeks adapted their alphabet, the direct ancestor of our own, from that used by the Phoenicians, the Mediterranean sea traders of antiquity. The Phoenician alphabet had introduced the novelty of employing

distinctive characters to represent the sounds of individual con-
sonants, and the Greeks added characters for vowel sounds as
well. Earlier systems had used a large number of characters to
represent entire syllables. The use of written characters with a
close relationship to the sounds of spoken language is generally
regarded as an advance over alternative writing systems employing relatively arbitrary symbols for entire words that represent meaning directly rather than through the sounds of speech.

The spoken language connection is seen as facilitating both
reading and writing, although it has considerable limitations.
And a substantial price was paid for the alphabetic principle in
that it always tied the writing system to a specific spoken language. People would not be able to read unless they *spoke*
the language that was the basis of a particular writing system.
This is currently a huge problem in China, where the government is attempting to introduce alphabetic writing. In the past,
all literate Chinese could write and read a common ideographic
system, in which symbols represented ideas, even though they
might not speak each other's language. In the same way, people
all over Europe and the Americas can understand $2 + 3 = 5$
without necessarily being able to understand "two plus three
equals five," "deux et trois font cinq," or "dos kai tessera einai
pende." Now the decision has been made in China that everyone who wants to be literate will have to understand Mandarin,
a language spoken in only part of the country.

Other difficulties result from tying the spelling of words to
sounds. Different varieties of English are spoken in different
regions of the United States, Canada, Britain, and other
English-speaking countries. Whose dialect should be selected
as the basis of the spelling system (partially abandoning the
phonetic principle for speakers of all other dialects)? Should
we all be permitted to spell according to the dialect we speak
(an inconceivable solution) or should we be expected to write
according to the dialect of our readers (an impossible alternative)?

Spoken languages also change over time. The very per-
manence of writing makes it incompatible with one of the major
features of all aspects of spoken language: constant change. If
the spelling system is to be fixed, for what particular time? Or
should it be changed at regular intervals? (The dynamic nature

of speech and the relative inflexibility of writing come into conflict in grammar and idiom too, leading to constant problems when people try to use written language as the standard to which appeals about proper usage are directed. Such people do not realize that written language always limps when spoken language leaps ahead.)

The old solution for all these difficulties was to allow spelling to vary freely, even for proper names. Shakespeare signed his name in a variety of ways. There was no means of achieving consistency, nor was there a demand for it, before the extensive development of the printing press. The printer's proofreader and the dictionary-maker were responsible for the arbitrary standardization of spelling. But the inevitable cost was a wide divergence between the way words were written and the way they were pronounced. Written language can never be an exact representation of speech.

How close does our alphabet and current system of spelling words permit us to get to the sounds of speech? The linguist Venezky (1970) made a computer analysis of twenty thousand common English words, a relatively small vocabulary. Every time the computer found a letter of the alphabet (or combination of letters, like *ph* or *ai*), representing a different sound, it counted this as a new *correspondence*. Thus the co-occurrence of the letter *c* with the sound /k/ in *cat* and with the sound /s/ in *city* counts as two correspondences (and the silent *c* at the beginning of *science* is a third). The result was over three hundred correspondences or "rules" for relating spelling and sound. Not one letter of the alphabet represented one sound exclusively, and not one sound of spoken language was represented uniquely by only one letter. The entire system is cumbersome. You need to know hundreds of rules (or large numbers of unpredictable exceptions) if you want to be able to "decode" the spelling of words to sounds. The system is also unreliable. If you apply all the rules you will on the average pronounce a word correctly only 25 percent of the time. And even if you do happen to decode a word correctly, you will not *know* that you have achieved this because none of the rules comes with a guarantee. Unless you know in advance how a word is spelled and pronounced, you will never be sure that you are pronouncing that particular word correctly. The entire rationale for *phonics*, which means teaching spelling-to-sound corre-spondence rules as a way of "decoding" unfamiliar words, is undermined.

None of this means that the spelling system of English is irrational or erratic. Spelling does not deserve the reputation it often has for being difficult or defective. The system may not represent the sounds of speech precisely, but that is not its main priority. The spelling of words usually reflects their meaning. Where sound and sense are in conflict—as they often are—spelling respects meaning. This principle explains why words like *medicine* and *medical* both have a *c* in them—not because *c* is sometimes pronounced /s/ and sometimes /k/ but because the two words share the same basic meaning. The principle explains the "silent" *g* in *sign* and *b* in *bomb*—not that the letters are intruding or performing some odd phonological func-tion, but because we would have to explain their sudden reap-pearance in *signature* and *bombard* if they were taken away. The best assumption upon meeting an unfamiliar word in read-ing is that it will share meaning with similarly spelled words but not necessarily share the same pronunciation.

In one sense, our writing system is far more consistent and less complex than speech. Words that sound alike frequently have different meanings (like *pair, pare,* and *pear; so, sow* and *sew*). But the alternative meanings are usually distinguished in the spelling—as in the examples I have just given.

It is true that other factors are involved in the spelling of many English words. Some spellings are based on false anal-ogies, a form of linguistic ignorance, like the mistaken assump-tion that the word now spelled *debt* had an origin similar to the word *debit* and should therefore have a *b* in it. Some spellings are the result of concern with legibility in the days when early printing techniques and typography made it difficult to discriminate among sequences of vertical letters like *l, m, n, i,* and *u*, so that the convention was established of spelling words like *love, front, women,* and *money* with *o* instead of *i* or *u*. Other conventions are purely orthographic, a quirk of spelling itself, like changing *-ie* to *-y* before adding *-ing* in words like *die* and *lie* to avoid long sequences of vowels like *dieing*. Some are grammatical, like always adding *s* (or *-es* if the spelling demands it) to make the plural of words that in spoken language might end in a /s/ sound (cats), /z/ (dogs), or /iz/ (fishes). Similarly, -ed is always added for a past tense suffix that might be pronounced /t/ (walked), /d/ (hugged), or /id/ (handed). But for all the incongruities, it is difficult to see where reformers of English spelling would begin without undermining its most powerful characteristic, the fact that it is in general consistent as far as the meaning of words is concerned. Almost all would-be reformers focus on making written language a closer representation of some idealized version of spoken language (not one spoken by any particular individual) at the cost of weakening its ties to meaning. An examination of the meaning-relatedness of English spelling led the linguists Chomsky and Halle (1968) to conclude that the present system is probably close to the optimum that could be achieved; any change would detract from its efficiency.

I would not want to claim that this relationship to meaning is the greatest virtue of the alphabet; I have several other candidates to present for that distinction. But the meaning relationship does have some extremely useful properties for reading and for writing—if only we could break free of the misconception that the only function of written letters is to represent the sounds of spoken words.

## Reading and learning to read

How much attention must we pay to the written or printed letters of the alphabet when we read? The answer is none at all if we are reading simply to comprehend, if the words we are looking at are familiar to us and we can make sense of them in context. The letters are there, but we recognize the words they are in as wholes, as total configurations (if indeed we need to identify individual words when we are reading entire phrases and sentences for meaning). We recognize words in the same way that we recognize faces, chairs and tables, animals and automobiles, not one bit at a time but all at once, as entities rather than as collections of parts. We read our words the way the Chinese read their ideographic symbols, as complete meaningful units. The letters are present, but only as elements in a whole. We no more read them one at a time than we examine individual bricks when we recognize a building.

Words are not *deciphered*; they are recognized. Written language is not *decoded into sound*, it has meaning brought to it. There is so much theoretical and experimental support for this point of view that it is impossible to summarize it in a paragraph or two in this essay. The entire argument can be found in my books *Understanding Reading* and *Reading Without Nonsense.*

An occasional objection to the preceding point of view is that whole-word recognition would place an intolerable burden on memory. Surely it is more economical to remember twenty six letters and their sounds than to remember many thousands of entire words? But apart from the fact that decoding from letters to sound is not a workable alternative—the basic undependability of phonics generalizations cannot be circumvented—it would in any case be too slow for reading with understanding. Reading letter by letter would place an intolerable burden upon short-term memory, upon our powers of concentration. In the time it takes to identify a single letter of the alphabet, an entire word or even group of words can be recognized, provided they make sense to us. Memory is not a problem. We remember many thousands of faces, places, animals, objects, and artifacts in our visual world, all of which we can distinguish at a glance (even though we may not be able to put a name to all of them). We remember many thousands of tastes, smells, sounds, textures, and other unique sensory qualities. We remember the sounds and meanings of tens of thousands of spoken words. The number of things that can be stored in the human brain seems to be limitless. *Memorization*—the deliberate effort to store something away for recall in the future—can sometimes be difficult, but that handicap is overcome by meaningfulness. Making sense of something usually means that we remember it, which explains how we can learn so much without awareness or conscious effort; it also explains why phonics rules are so difficult for beginning readers to learn—the rules do not make sense to them. *Recall* is another, separate problem of memory. Putting something into the brain may not give as much trouble as getting it out when we want it. But again this problem is solved by meaningfulness—we recall best when we are in a situation where there are many clues, many avenues, to what we want to recall. Even children find it easier to recognize words in a story that makes sense to them than to recognize the same words in isolation.

What about words we have never seen before? Surely then phonics is required? But the decoding alternative still is not feasible, no matter how desirable we think it might be. Decoding to sound is the last resort when fluent readers meet an unfamiliar word. The best clues lie in the general *context*, where the meaning of the whole can suggest the identity of a particular word, and in words that are already known. Words that look alike tend to have the same meaning; you may not have seen the word *telefacture* before (I think I just invented it), but if you know *telephone* and *manufacture* then not only can you identify the new word, you can make a reasonable guess as to a possible meaning. Of course it can be argued that phonics is relevant, that context may tell you that the name of a car is involved but not whether it is Ford or Chevrolet. Surely it helps to know that Chevrolet could not begin with an *F*? But distinguishing two words in this way is not decoding to sound, it is selecting among alternative possibilities, a completely different matter. Phonics looks much more efficient when the number of possibilities is limited and it is not necessary to sound out the entire word.

What about learning to read? Don't children need to know the sounds of the letters? Once again the system does not work (except in the highly artificial "beginning reader" situation where nonsense like "Nan can fan Dan" is concocted to make phonics look efficient). The first words children learn to read, like their names and those of their friends, where they live, and various well-advertised commodities, are never taught to them on the basis of the sounds of the letters. As they acquire a repertoire of known words, children are able to recognize and even capitalize upon the relationship that letters have with sounds. But the children who are to become fluent readers will use the same strategies with unfamiliar words as more experienced readers —they will use the clues of context and their own knowledge of similar words to reduce their uncertainty about the new ones. There is no need to conceal from children the relationships of letters to sounds, but there is no need to impose rules either. Understanding of the utility and limitations of phonics comes with reading, and what children need initially is help with reading, not phonics instruction, as members of the literacy club.

## Writing and learning to write

Or course, there is much more to writing, and to learning to write, than spelling, despite the emphasis put on that particular subject at school. But because my current concern is concentrated upon the alphabet, I shall confine myself in this essay to the subject of spelling.

If we had no alphabet we could not spell. Precision in writing would be a matter of something else, like the drawing of conventional pictographs or ideograms. Drawing is involved in producing handwritten alphabetical letters, but our system of writing demands something more, it demands knowledge of how letters are put together in the form of words, of how words are spelled. How do we learn to spell all of the written words we use (or most of them, at least)? Once again there are two main points of view. One view maintains that we use our knowledge of spelling-to-sound correspondences (now reversed into sound-to-spelling correspondences) to construct the spelling of every word when we need it, or at least to provide those spellings we don't happen to have learned. This view relies upon the familiar argument that it would place an intolerable load on memory to store away every single spelling we might require. The opposite point of view also presents the familiar arguments that remembering spellings is not an impossible burden (unless they are presented to children by means of meaningless spelling lists, exercises, and flashcards), and that rules of spelling would not work, even if we could remember them all—and all the exceptions. A group of researchers (Hanna, Hodges, and Hanna, 1971) cunningly reversed the procedure of Venezky that I mentioned earlier. They programmed their own computer with over two hundred correspondence rules derived from an analysis of seventeen thousand common words, and then instructed it to *spell* those words (from a phonetic representation of their pronunciation) by using the correspondence rules. Not only was the computer right only half the time—or wrong half the time, depending upon how you look at it—but there was never any assurance when it was right. In other words, even if the rules happen to give the correct spelling, you still have to confirm it elsewhere and remember it for the next time. You are no better off.

Spelling is not a matter of writing down the sounds of words.

Foke hoo rite fonetikly are the worst spellers. Most of us are obliged to write phonetically occasionally, when we have no other resource—for example in writing a name that we have heard but have never seen in print—and we know how bizarre and inaccurate such invented attempts usually are. Children at the beginning of their writing careers are frequently in the same position—they just do not know enough correct spellings, so they use the best resource available to them. They invent spellings to serve for the time being. Going to a dictionary or asking someone whenever they need a spelling is too time-consuming. Some researchers have been so impressed by the ingenuity and acute phonetic discernment displayed by children in this way that they refer to invented spelling as a "stage" children must go through, as if it were some kind of special mental state, an inevitable aspect of immaturity. But the children are doing nothing that more experienced writers do not do, except that they have to do it more often. They know that conventionally "correct" spellings exist, but they also know that they do not know them yet, so they do the best they can.

Learning to spell is not a matter of writing down the sounds of words or of employing scores of spelling rules—it is a matter of discovering and remembering proper spellings. The alphabet no more helps writers to spell words on the basis of their sounds than it enables readers to sound out words on the basis of their spelling. Spelling does not come from writing at all, but from reading. We learn the spelling of words the way we learn their punctuation and meaning in spoken language, by experiencing them in a meaningful context. What writing does for us, and for children in particular, is facilitate the kind of reading that I call *reading like a writer*, when we read not just to comprehend, but as if we ourselves were writing what we read. As a consequence we learn spellings, punctuation, capitalization, and everything else that is distinctive about written language at the time when it is most relevant to us.

The best thing for children who are not yet very experienced spellers is not to have their opportunities to write denied while they are subjected to pointless drills or exercises in alphabetic correspondences, but to be helped to get on with the satisfying business of writing without frustration over exactitude in spelling, which, as I have argued in the preceding essay, will come with reading. (See also *Writing and the Writer* [Smith, 1982b], for more about writing in general and about the spelling issues discussed in this essay.)

## Advantages of the alphabet

The final defense of phonics is sometimes the existence of the alphabet itself. Why should there be an alphabet if the letters and their relationships to sound have so little relevance in actual reading and writing? But our alphabetic system has at least four marked advantages that make it quite unnecessary to find mythical justifications for its existence. The advantages of the alphabet are that it gives us (1) a way of talking about written language; (2) a means of memorizing written words; (3) easy reproduction, by people and by technology; and (4) a way of organizing the world.

### TALKING ABOUT WRITING

Imagine trying to tell someone how to write a word if you could not refer to the alphabet. Could you explain that *house* is drawn from left to right with two upright strokes and a crossbar, a circle, a vertical oval open at the top, and so on? How would you explain the difference between *their* and *there* if you could not refer to the letters? Imagine the reverse—someone trying to ask you to identify an unknown word by describing its shape to you. With the alphabet, *talking* about written language is easy. The way to draw the word *house* is to write down H-O-U-S-E. The way to inquire about the uncertain word is to ask what T-H-E-I-R spells. With the alphabet, you no longer need to *show* written words to discuss them; you can easily put them into spoken language. That is an advantage that no other form of script has, and it plays a part in all of the other advantages that I have yet to discuss. It is probably easier to talk about written words than about any other object in the visual world. I could not describe a face, or a tree, or an animal, with such precision.

The advantage of knowing the alphabet is that it gives children a way of talking about written language. If you cannot talk about something, it is very difficult to learn about it, especially if you must depend a good deal on knowledge possessed by other people. The alphabet offers power and control, even to the beginner. You gain in confidence and in competence when you can talk about what you are doing.

MEMORIZATION OF WRITTEN WORDS

The fact that we can describe how written words appear means that it is easier to remember how to reproduce them. To recognize a word in reading we must remember how it looks, in the same way that we remember the faces that we are able to recognize. But being able to recall how someone or something looks is not the same thing as being able to reproduce the image; we need some kind of description so that we do not make mistakes in detail. I can recognize my home from all angles, but if you asked me to draw the side wall I would have to *calculate* how many windows there are. I need a description. To be able to confirm to ourselves the spelling of all the thousands of words that we can spell, we must remember descriptions of those spellings. The alphabet enables us to remember complete and unambiguous descriptions of every written word.

The problem with ideographic written languages like Chinese is not that they are a strain on readers; it is no more difficult to remember how a word *looks*, whether alphabetic or otherwise, than to remember a face. The problem is to remember how the word should be reproduced, a problem for the writer. Children learn to read Chinese as quickly as they learn to read English, but writing Chinese is a much more complex proposition. It would be difficult for me to remember how to draw a particular house, or to draw the appropriate symbol in Chinese script, but for English writing all I need remember is H-O-U-S-E. If something can be talked about in simple terms, it can be remembered and recalled in simple terms.

REPRODUCTION BY PEOPLE AND BY TECHNOLOGY

The fact that written words can be broken down into a small set of nameable parts is not simply an advantage when we want to talk about them. It also means that written words are easier to reproduce. They are easier to *draw*. There is no need to practice and remember how to draw hundreds of complicated figures—just the twenty-six soldiers of the alphabet. If you can draw those twenty-six letters then you can write any of the words in the language (provided you can remember or find out the spelling).

Breaking down written words into a couple of dozen simple elements bestows enormous power on people wanting to reproduce them by hand. For mechanical reproduction, the alphabet opened up a whole new realm of opportunities; it made possible the printing presses of Gutenberg and Caxton. The use and reuse of "movable" pieces of type, each corresponding to a letter, was the basis of their technology. Printing existed for hundreds of years before the alphabet, but until words could be reduced to letters, books and manuscripts had to be reproduced entire pages at a time. Pages were reproduced like pictures.

Shortage of suitable paper had a great deal to do with the painfully slow development of printing after the invention of the alphabet. But the spread of literacy from the sixteenth century until the last few decades—when a different technology again revolutionized text reproduction—would not have been achieved had the alphabet not existed. It is interesting to reflect that photographic technology now makes dependence on individual letters unnecessary, and that printing is once more being done in the only way it was once possible, by the reproduction of entire pages at a time.

It was not only because an infinity of possible books could be produced combining a few basic elements that the alphabet was so productive for technology. There was also the fact that all the elements of writing could be controlled easily from keyboards manipulated at great speed by just two hands. A major reason for recent Japanese and Chinese decisions to convert to an alphabetic script, despite the initial *reduction* in literacy that will follow, was that the traditional ideographic systems, with their multiplicity of complex symbols, cannot conveniently be placed on the keyboard of a typewriter (and later on that of a computer). The Japanese and Chinese still work primarily in English on their computers because of the demands of the keyboard.

There are two other factors that I want to mention under this general heading of reproduction, even though in other contexts they would warrant extended discussion in their own right. The first is related to standardization, to conformity even. A distinctive characteristic of the ideograph is that its meaning is never fixed; there is no ultimate court of appeal. One individual might argue that a certain symbol stands for justice, another that it really means truth, and a third, perhaps, might say right thinking. With alphabetic systems such a dispute could not exist. A written word can be related to spoken language immediately, and there the entire argument might end. Perhaps this is a good thing. It could be significant, I think, that the alphabet was promoted by the Phoenicians, who were merchants. Presumably they wanted a system that would not be open to interpretation, where every text unarguably represented what it was supposed to represent, bills of account and deeds of ownership, no matter what language or dialect the reader spoke or how much time had elapsed since the writing. Is what is good for business good for more abstract concepts like justice, truth, or beauty? This is not the place to enter such a debate, but I find it interesting that when the Koreans decided to alphabetize their writing system, they chose to retain ideographs for several hundred concepts of the kind I have just mentioned, recognizing that you do not necessarily understand what a word means by being able to put a name to it.

My other general point has to do with legibility. For some reason not adequately explored, written words composed from the limited set of letters of an alphabet are particularly *discriminable*. For most of us, with or without our spectacles, it is easier to read words (on signs and billboards) at a distance than it is to recognize faces. Words flashed briefly on a screen are easier to identify than pictures of the objects they name. Observers respond more quickly in saying "house" or "tree," and make fewer mistakes, when the words *HOUSE* or *TREE* are flashed to them than when they are shown a picture or drawing of a house or a tree. They even say *blue* or *green* faster when presented with the word than when their entire field of view is suddenly filled with the color. Clearly, the alphabet has some special visual properties.

ORGANIZING THE WORLD

We not only have an alphabet, we also have alphabetical order. Aleph, the original Hebrew name for the first letter of the alphabet, also means "ox." In its original form the letter was the other way up, rather like our V with a horizontal line across the middle, and it looks a little like the skull and horns of a bull. It is also similar to the configuration of stars that gives the name to the constellation of the bull (Taurus) in the zodiac. In the times when the alphabet was being developed, Taurus heralded spring, the beginning of the year, and was therefore listed first among the twelve constellations of the zodiac. It may have been thought that the sequence of letters should also begin with the bull, so that the notion of a special order has always been part of our alphabet.

The alphabet helps to keep things straight and under control. This also may have appealed to the Phoenicians for their commercial purposes. I think I am not stretching the point too far if I suggest that contemporary Western culture would have been impossible without the existence of alphabetical order. How would we consult our libraries, dictionaries, encyclopedias, and telephone books if entries were included randomly or in some other kind of order (as in the yellow pages or street directories)? It has been impossible for the Chinese to construct a *convenient* dictionary of their own language or a manageable telephone book, as anyone who has visited China will attest. Another interesting indication, I think, is that it is the bureaucrats in China who have been promoting alphabetization, not the literati or school teachers. Imagine trying to conduct a census—or to collect taxes on a large scale—if names could not be easily organized on a list.

## Conclusions

My purpose in preparing this essay was twofold. I wanted to show that the alphabetic nature of our written language does not necessarily entail that the correspondences existing between the spelling of written words and their sounds in speech have great relevance to reading and writing. In particular, I was concerned that the importance of phonics in reading instruction and in spelling was overrated, and that emphasis on these aspects of the alphabet could be greatly disadvantageous to learners. But I also wanted to highlight alternative advantages of the alphabet that are less frequently considered. I did not want to say that the alphabet was useless, only that its major value might lie elsewhere than it is generally put.

I would not like to judge which is the most important of the

four broad categories of advantage that I have distinguished—
talking about written language, memorizing, reproducing, or
organizing. Different aspects might well have different values
for different people. But collectively they have an enormous
utility, more than enough to justify the presence of the alphabet
and the need to learn it, in conventional order.

I have been very practical. I have talked only of the uses of
the alphabet, not of its delights. I have not reflected upon the
beauty and endless variety of our twenty-six soldiers, of illu-
minated letters, typefonts, and typography. There can be harmonies and subtleties in print that are surely the equal of those
found in music, or at least in the human voice. The alphabet
is one of the ornaments of civilization, a jewel of human invention. More is the pity then that we make it so drab, and
employ it so misguidedly, in education.

# Learning to be a critical thinker

**4** I share a growing concern in education today about critical thinking. Children do not do enough critical thinking. They appear not to know how to do it. The situation should be remedied forthwith. With all of this I agree. To say that the entire world could benefit from an increase in critical thinking might not be an understatement. It is a disgrace and a disaster that students of all ages are not exercising more critical thought than they do in our schools.

But when I examine in detail what is widely perceived to be the problem and its solution, I find myself in frequent disagreement. Many who assert that more critical thinking is needed do not express very clearly what they think critical thinking is or how they expect it to be demonstrated. They make reference to reasoning, inference, problem solving, prediction, expression, abstract thought, concept formation, and classification, to anything *except* perhaps critical thinking. They seem to regard these aspects of mental activity as distinct *skills*, which I think is misleading. They believe children lack them, which is false. They assert that the "skills" can be taught, which is simplistic, and that systematic instruction is the way to teach them, which is wrong. They apparently feel that children do not normally think, and that this is because they have failed to learn something. My view, on the contrary, is that children are skilled and practiced thinkers, with intellectual powers that have been submerged in the course of their education, and that efforts to teach critical thinking in systematic ways will only perpetuate the conditions that have created the problem. To drill children in the skills of critical thinking is like increasing the dosage for someone who is allergic to a drug and who had no need for it in the first place.

In this essay I shall first inquire into the nature of critical thinking, especially in terms of the particular inadequacies that children are supposed to manifest. I shall then outline evidence that children demonstrate precisely the kinds of thinking they are supposed to lack and go on to consider why it should suddenly appear in their school years that they have lost, or never had, such ability. After examining what might have gone wrong with education, I shall suggest how it could be put right. The problem is not insoluble, only difficult. Before leaping to conclusions that might aggravate the situation we should demonstrate critical thinking ourselves.

## What is critical thinking?

The linguist Halliday (1973) made the profound observation that children do not learn spoken language as a system, as a generalizable set of skills, which they then apply to a variety of uses. Language is always used for a purpose. Children learn language and its uses simultaneously, says Halliday, and for any uses of language with which they are not familiar they will appear not to have language. I have gone further and argued that it is through its uses that children learn language, both spoken and written. Language can never be separated from its uses, and its uses are multitudinous.

In a quietly reasoned analysis entitled *Critical Thinking and Education*, John McPeck (1981) reaches conclusions remarkably similar to Halliday's with respect to critical thinking. He points out that thinking always has a subject—we always think about *something*—and that being unable to think about something in a particular manner indicates unfamiliarity with the subject matter rather than an underlying inadequacy of thought itself. If an activity or state of affairs is totally unfamiliar to us, if we cannot think about it at all, then there is no way we can think about it critically.

Consider the example of automobile mechanics, an area in which my own ignorance could scarcely be exaggerated. If my car stalls I have no idea what to do beyond checking the gas gauge and trying the ignition switch again. But I will not remedy my inadequacy by taking a course on critical thinking. A mechanic recently told me that my carburetor was hanging loose. For all I knew he was paying me a compliment. I could not infer from his statement whether immediate action was required or if I should anticipate hazards in the future. I assume this does not mean that something is wrong with my powers of inference or my ability to predict. The trouble is my unfamiliarity with automobile engines. We can only infer, predict, and think critically with respect to specific subject matter, and if a subject is foreign to us then we will not be able to demonstrate any thinking ability. This seems to me identical with the language situation. We cannot talk comprehensibly about anything we do not understand, no matter how extensive our language abilities. There are no higher-order language or thinking skills that cover all situations.

Like many theorists, McPeck distinguishes critical thinking from logic, both formal and informal. Being logical does not guarantee that problems will be solved, and successful problem solvers do not necessarily proceed on the basis of logic. For a start, logic is concerned only with the validity of an argument, not with its truth or relevance. A syllogism may be logical but not true, and decisions about truth depend upon relevant knowledge of the world and our values.

McPeck also argues that critical thinking (like "language") is not generalizable. Thinking critically is the way a particular thing is done, like singing a song sensitively. We can think about innumerable things critically, which means that we can think critically in innumerable ways. In a significant analogy McPeck compares the alternative view with that which tries to reduce learning to read to a matter of acquiring a few basic skills. The word "skill" is extensively misused in education. There is a tendency to define everything to be learned in terms of skills —reading skills, comprehension skills, creativity and prediction skills—as if they were in the same category as physical skills like swimming and running. It is a false and misleading metaphor. Physical activities involve muscular strength and coordination, which may indeed improve with exercise and drills. But as Krashen (1984) points out, the development of language and other cognitive abilities depends on understanding, not practice. There are no patterns of activity in the brain to be strengthened or coordinated so that we can think better.

McPeck's conclusion is that critical thinking is a disposition rather than a skill, a tendency to behave in a particular way on particular occasions. He sees this disposition as one of "reflective skepticism"—the judicious suspension of assent, readiness to consider alternative explanations, not taking anything for granted when it might be reasonable to doubt (all of which again requires a broad understanding of subject matter). One might argue about the specifics of McPeck's definition, but it underlines two important points. The demonstration of critical thinking requires a willingness to behave in a particular way on occasions when one knows what one is talking about, and it must frequently be a challenge to conventional ways of thought.

OTHER ASPECTS OF THINKING

More generally, all of the terms used to describe various aspects of thinking are concerned with relationships. The terms overlap in use, so that exact definitions are not possible. But as a rough approximation it might be said that *reasoning* refers to relationships within a series of statements or state of affairs; one thing follows another. Thus in language we might reason that an argument is valid if a conclusion is coherently related to its premises, and an automobile mechanic might reason that an engine is faulty if the valve timing is not properly synchronized with the ignition system. *Inference* involves relationships among particular statements or states of affairs and some more general circumstances, while *problem solving* relates existing states of affairs to desired states, and *prediction* relates existing to future states of affairs. *Classification, categorization, concept formation* and other manifestations of *higher-order* or *abstract* thinking all impose relationships upon statements or states of affairs.

In short, all of these different aspects of thinking concern relationships, linking things in particular ways, and all depend upon specific knowledge of how things are necessarily or conventionally related. It does not make sense to talk about a general ability to produce or understand complex relationships—good writers are not necessarily good chess players or good automobile mechanics.

All of the aspects of thought I have mentioned are in fact dispositions to act in a particular way in situations where there is already a general understanding. How can any useful aspect of thought be demonstrated where there is bewilderment or confusion? But there are other factors as well that determine whether appropriate thinking is demonstrated. One might be termed interest, though interest and experience are closely related. We are unlikely to demonstrate sustained thinking in situations that are boring to us or that we do not find relevant in some way. Another factor is our self-concept; we are unlikely to behave in particular ways if we do not see ourselves as the kind of person who behaves in these ways—what I have referred to as "being a member of the club." Finally, we are unlikely to do anything we think inappropriate for us. We may suspect we know more about our automobile engine than the mechanic, but we will be reluctant to assert this if we feel it is not our place to do so, if the mechanic has the authority.

In summary, critical thinking and all the other commonly distinguished aspects of thought are dispositions rather than skills. They are not generalizable. Their demonstration depends upon familiarity with the subject, experience, interest, expectation, self-image, and a sense of what is appropriate.

## Children and thinking

There is extensive evidence that every child is disposed and able to behave in precisely the ways that are characterized as critical thinking, both specifically (reflective skepticism) and more generally (in manipulating all manner of relationships). It is by thinking in such ways that children learn.

All children without gross and obvious physical, mental, or social handicaps accomplish at least three enormous feats of learning in the first few years of their lives. They learn the language around them, they learn the culture they are in, and they learn to make sense of the physical world as it impinges upon them. None of this understanding is inherited in the sense that specific knowledge is encoded in the genes. The language children learn depends on where they are brought up, not on who their parents are. Every one of us when we were born could have learned any language in the world, and would have done so, effortlessly, if we had spent our first few years among speakers of the language. Indeed, since language changes all the time, babies are born with the ability to learn languages that do not yet exist—a mind-boggling intellectual power.

As I outlined in the opening essay, by the age of four every child has mastered an extensive vocabulary and a complete grammar, not the idealized vocabulary and grammar we might like the child to be able to speak in school but the actual vocabulary and grammar of family and friends in the language community to which the child belongs.

Children learn to use language idiomatically (which by definition is the way language is actually spoken), and idiom cannot be predicted from vocabulary and grammar. Children lean subtle rules of cohesion, by which statements are interlocked and related to external contexts, and they learn to respect intricate demands of register, which determine the appropriate way to discuss particular things in particular circumstances with particular people. They learn intonation, gesture, eye contact, facial expression, and the appropriate distance to stand from other people when talking with them (all of which vary according to intricate relationships of status). All these complex aspects of language are conventional, differing from one community, society, and culture to another (in part because these differences are the way in which communities distinguish themselves). All have to be learned.

Children do not simply learn to talk like the people around them. They learn to eat, drink, walk, dress, groom, and ornament themselves as others do in the groups to which they belong. They learn interests and values, expectations and imperatives. They learn their own identity, their place in the world as they see it and as it is seen by other people. They learn all the things that are conventional, including the ways in which to affiliate themselves with others and the ways in which to express their own uniqueness. Every social group has its own conventions, expectations, and ways of looking at the world. Yet every baby learns precisely that culture into which he or she is accepted as belonging. Every child is born with the ability to learn any culture in the word, including cultures that do not yet exist.

Even the physical facts of the world have to be learned, including those we think most obvious. Nothing in the world announces itself—we once had to learn that rain is wet, that fire burns, that birds fly and fish swim, that night follows day, that behavior has consequences, and that people have all kinds of personal and public relationships with each other. Everything we take for granted today in the complex world in which we live is a legacy of something we learned in the past.

Anthropologists, sociologists, and psychologists have recently accumulated a mass of evidence that children in many cultures discover a great deal about reading and writing before they come to school, without any instruction, often without anyone being aware of what they have learned (Goelman, Oberg, and Smith, 1984).

None of this learning is deliberately planned, either by the child or by the people around the child. None of it is organized. There are no objectives, guidelines, lesson plans, instructional sequences, drills, exercises, assignments, scores, or tests. Learning occurs as it makes sense and is relevant to the learner and is taken for granted by the learner and the groups to which the learner belongs.

Babies learn to understand the language spoken around them, and to speak it themselves, when they are admitted into a club of users of that language. Experienced members of this club demonstrate all the club activities to new members—they show what language is used for—and they help newcomers to use language for their own purposes. There are no prerequisites for membership in such clubs, just mutual unqualified acceptance. The child and the more experienced club members see each other as the same kind of people. It is taken for granted on both sides that the child will learn but also that not everyone will be as experienced and practiced as everyone else.

How exactly does the learning take place? The child learns by critical thinking in specific situations, relating behavior to intentions. This is no trivial matter of habit formation or imitation. A parent says "Here's a drink for you" and offers the child a drink, and from understanding the intentions behind the utterances, the child learns a little more about language and its relationship to events. A child hears one person comment to another that it is raining outside and learns a few more things about vocabulary, grammar, register, idiom, intonation, and other aspects of language. Innumerable times a day, every day of the year, the child learns more about language, about culture, about the world, so effortlessly that we rarely suspect how much learning is taking place. And it all involves inference, prediction, problem solving, reasoning, categorization, and concept formation—abstract thought of the highest order relating statements or states of affairs to contexts and purposes.

All of this learning involves critical thinking, a reflective skepticism, never taking anything for granted. An infant might often get the right result for the wrong reason. A hypothesis that large animals with four legs are horses is fine until the first cow is encountered, when the hypothesis must be modified. It is discovered that adding /s/ or /z/ to words makes them plural—until the child says "childs." Children must always be ready to change their mind. All knowledge must be tentative, neither clung to blindly nor abandoned prematurely. Everything must be questioned, including one's own beliefs.

I think it likely that the power of children's thought will be increasingly recognized and even utilized by societies in the future. Children's ability to understand and learn new languages and new cultures is already being demonstrated with respect to computers, whose unexplored potential tends to defeat less adventurous thinkers. In any school with computers, students are the experts, and teachers must at last acknowledge that they learn from students.

A confused child does not learn. The problem is not that the child cannot learn or cannot think but that the child is confused. No one can learn in a situation where nothing makes sense; there is nothing to learn except that the situation does not make sense. The natural reaction to situations that are confusing, where there is nothing to learn, is to escape. Boredom and distraction ensure that we do not waste time not learning in the same adaptive way that the feeling of suffocation ensures that we always breathe. Children who are confused do not need additional learning skills or thinking skills, they need help to find sense and relevance in the situation they are in—provided of course that the situation has sense and relevance. Children who appear to have difficulty learning have an even greater need for situations to be made comprehensible to them.

Children who lack experience of particular kinds of situations do not learn, but again the problem and its solution are—or should be—obvious. The problem is lack of experience, not inability to learn or to think. In addition, children will not demonstrate the ability to think if they do not believe that thinking in the particular circumstances is possible or permissible for them. They are not members of the club. If their self-image is that they cannot think critically, if they do not think it worthwhile, or if they are persuaded that it is not their place to think critically in the circumstances, then they will not appear to think. (And others who are not able to think critically about the situation may conclude that the children have not learned to think critically.) But once again, the children do not lack general skills, and efforts to teach such skills can only result in more failure and frustration.

## Thinking and school

If children demonstrate such powerful learning and thinking ability in the first few years of their lives, why do they not continue to do so when they arrive in school? I shall pick up two points from my earlier discussion and ask two blunt questions.

- Children learn when they have opportunities and reason to use language and critical thinking personally. *When is critical thinking useful to children in school?*
- Children learn from what is demonstrated to them, from what they see others doing. *When do students see teachers engaging in critical thinking in the classroom?*

STUDENTS AND CRITICAL THINKING

Is it a caricature to say that when children first arrive in school they are greeted with the good news that they no longer need worry about finding things out for themselves? All they need do is learn what the teacher says they ought to know.

The longer the child stays in school, the more rigid and conforming the child's experience is likely to be. The constraint typically begins early in the primary grades, ironically with reading instruction. And tragically, it tends to be most marked for children identified as most at risk.

I am talking about what I call programmatic instruction, which I have discussed in detail in *Insult to Intelligence* (Smith, 1986). Programs come in a variety of guises, not always clearly labeled "program," but they always include a predetermined sequence of "skills" for the child to learn, exercises and drills through which the learning is supposed to take place, and frequent tests to ensure that the learning has occurred. This is nothing like the way children learn about language, culture, and the world outside school. It is the antithesis of learning through thinking. There is no immediate meaning or utility to the child in any of it, beyond the fact that there is "work" to be done. The learning situations are decontextualized, fragmented, and trivial, which is the opposite of the circumstances in which innate thinking ability can flourish. Programs are *devised* to prevent children from employing their own judgment; some programs boast that they are "guessproof," that they are essentially meaningless.

The people who construct and promote such programs take upon themselves the awesome responsibility of deciding what children whom they cannot see should be forced to learn next—at the cost of more meaningful experience. There is no evidence that any skills program has ever made a child literate, but the only consequence of this failure has been further pressure on teachers to employ more programs and rely less on their own insights and teaching abilities. Indeed, teaching has often come to be seen as a matter of administering programs. Programs deprive children of opportunities to see language and thought used in meaningful contexts with the result that children, teachers, parents, and professors of education alike have become persuaded that the most important part of learning is the marks you get. There is little recognition that activities are made artificial and pointless so that they can be easily "evaluated," under the mistaken notion that it is only through "scores" that quality control can be exercised in education.

There is no point in being sentimental about all this and saying that of course children get opportunities to think in the classroom; why else should we have schools? Teachers must look critically at what goes on in classrooms. This is not something that they are often trained to do in their own preparation by college professors who themselves seem often to think that what matters is the scores obtained on tasks and tests, in their own classrooms and those of their students. Students are not thinking critically when they work their way through an activity sheet, a workbook, a set of questions on a decontextualized piece of text, a small set-piece of writing on some ritual topic, exercises, drills, or tests, even if whatever they are working on is prominently labeled "comprehension" or some other idealized objective and accompanied by glowing testimonials. The growing concern with teaching "consumerism" to children is ironic when so little discrimination is exercised in the purchase of classroom materials for use with children. Once again one might ask what is demonstrated.

No one benefits from this mania for marking and emphasis on skills-based programs. Children who succeed would do well in any case, since they are probably already experienced in what the activity purports to teach them, like the children who are readers and can therefore make sense of the phonics drills. But even these children can quickly learn that reading and writing are not meaningful and productive activities but decontextualized classroom tasks, worth doing only for the grades they bring. By making all the tasks and tests look good, such children help perpetuate the myth that programs successfully teach.

The children who pay the price and suffer the damage of drills and tests are the ones who do poorly. They quickly become persuaded that they are not "readers," "writers," or "thinkers," whatever it is they are supposed to be failing to do, and they are effectively excluded from the clubs of people who do these things. The inner strength and external support that are essential for learning are denied to them. They have even less opportunity to experience club activity in any meaningful context and are forced to struggle even harder to learn blindly. But little of this can be explained to those already convinced that "basic skills" must be taught before anyone can engage in any meaningful learning and activity. It would be a mockery to attempt to teach critical thinking in circumstances that directly preclude it.

TEACHERS AND CRITICAL THINKING

Where can children see critical thinking demonstrated in school? I do not mean teachers telling them how to answer questions on worksheets, but teachers actually engaging in "reflective skepticism," suspending assent to some program or test, considering alternatives, behaving like members of the club and showing what critical thinking can be used for. Teachers may be further removed from the daily practice of critical thinking than the children they are supposed to teach. I am not offering this as a criticism of teachers, who, I maintain, should be given control of their classrooms and the autonomy to educate the children they know in the way they think most relevant and appropriate. But teachers as well as students are victims of the stultification of thought in education.

The hardest task I had as a professor in university faculties of education was to get graduate students, qualified teachers all, to think and write critically. In researching, summarizing, and presenting what other people had written their competence was exemplary. They were outstanding at elaborating upon the implications of other people's theories for classroom practice. But when I asked for an argument, they had little idea how to do it. They were excellent at "furthermore" but weak at "on the other hand." If I asked for two sides of an argument I got opposing points of view with no effort to choose between them. Another "expert" would have to decide. If I required students to argue a position persuasively (which I thought they would have to do in the world outside), they told me what they "believed." If I said I was not convinced, they revised it to "strongly believed."

These experienced teachers undervalued their own thought. It was not their place to argue with experts, with people more senior in the hierarchy, even though they—the teachers—had the experience in the classroom. One told me it was rude to criticize. Another said she had not written an essay on an excellent idea of her own because she could not find an "authority" to credit with the idea. Many said they had no experience in writing a critical essay arguing their own point of view. No one had ever asked for one, and previous attempts had been rejected as "unscholarly." Some students, perhaps desperate to please, submitted papers consisting almost entirely of clearly labeled excerpts from my own writing. When I gave them low marks they said I was failing myself.

Where had these teachers—among the brightest and most dedicated members of their profession—learned to think (or not to think) in this way? Part of the problem is the notion that education is the "acquisition of information," perhaps the first thing demonstrated to children. The student's job is to find out what other people know, whether in first grade or graduate school, especially when they are conveniently told what they are supposed to learn (which is regarded as the essence of good teaching). When I asked my graduate students why I should tell them what they were supposed to know when they had so much more experience of teaching their subjects and grade level, I was told it was my role to prepare them for the tests they had to take. In such a context, to be encouraged to have their own ideas was counterproductive for them. If that is a graduate student's perception of the student-teacher relationship, what must a grade school student feel?

I do not think any of these inadequacies on the part of my students could be attributed to a lack of general critical thinking skills. These students would not have been helped by courses on inference or problem solving. Their handicap was that they did not see themselves as members of the club of critical thinkers in education. They had been taught to rely on programs, on what they had been told to read or on what the experts said. And like their own students, my students had learned what they were taught, what was demonstrated to them.

When I challenged my university colleagues that our education programs set terrible examples—when I recommended that we replace half the content area courses and graded activities with opportunities for independent observation, reading, thinking, and arguing—I was reminded that we were preparing teachers for the way schools operated. We were giving schools what they wanted. This is the defense of publishers when they are criticized for producing so much rubbish in the name of "educational materials." They would not publish it if schools did not buy it. There is no point in waiting for publishers or college professors to reform education.

## Toward the solution

Children may exhibit little critical thinking in school, not because they are incapable but because they have little opportunity to do so. When they are required to engage in what is called critical thinking, the activities tend to make small sense to them. Children lack demonstrations of critical thinking in action, and this lack cannot be repaired by drilling them in critical-thinking exercises, giving them puzzles, or subjecting them to batteries of critical thinking tests. Schools—and schools of education—require radical change so that they become places where critical thinking takes place constantly and naturally, by teachers and by students. Learning and critical thinking should be taken for granted in the way it is taken for granted that everyone in a club will engage in the activities of that club and help newcomers to participate.

I have two general suggestions about how this end might be

achieved. The first involves what I have called *enterprises* as illustrations of the kinds of environment in which children naturally use (and learn) reading and writing. The other is more direct—and more political.

## ENGAGEMENT IN ENTERPRISES

Two examples of enterprises for all grade levels are running a newspaper and building a shed. Both entail reading, writing and computation, planning, organization, prediction, problem solving, initiative, imagination, collaboration, management, and fitness of purpose (as opposed to abstract "marking"). Other possibilities range from writing letters on relevant topics to relevant people, devising and producing diets and menus, and publishing directories and reviews to major construction and design projects, wherever possible contributing to broader communities outside the school. All can involve numbers of individuals of differing degrees of experience and ability working collaboratively over extended periods of time. These are merely examples. Scores of alternatives exist.

In themselves, enterprises may not sound particularly novel, and indeed they should not be regarded as unusual or exotic. Enterprises should be distinctive because they are engaged in for their own sake. Participation is voluntary and no one receives formal credit for engaging in them, whether students or teachers. The utility of engaging in enterprises must be obvious—they are "clubs." There are no restrictions on the basis of age, grade level, experience, or ability. In fact enterprises should deliberately reach across classroom barriers and break down the distinction between teachers and students. There are no academic roles in clubs.

Enterprises are possibilities for meaningful environments in which children can become literate, but I see no reason why the prescriptions should be changed if children are to engage in critical thought rather than in meaningful learning—the two are inseparable. Schools should be learning emporia.

Many teachers cannot imagine school activities without evaluation. But getting a mark does nothing for learning or for critical thinking. Children who refuse to "work" unless there is a grade show what they have learned: that they see no intrinsic purpose or value in what goes on at school. I have had graduate students make the same objection to ungraded assignments. The teacher's role is not to recruit students into enterprises but to ensure that there are enterprises sufficiently open and rewarding that engagement takes place. Where can the time be found for enterprises? Ideally, from all of the time that is currently dedicated to programs. But in practice, enterprises may have to be the wedge that teachers begin to insert in the structure of programmatic instruction to break it open. Everything depends on the imagination and initiative of individual teachers who have faith in children. In Victoria, one group of kindergarten children wrote, composed, choreographed, produced, and performed its own opera.

CRITICAL THINKING IN ACTION

My second suggestion is directly pertinent. Sometimes after I have talked about the conflict in education between teachers and programs I am challenged to be specific about what teachers might do on Monday morning that would be different. My response is always "Talk about the conflict with your students —whatever their age." The one thing that is not discussed openly in school is education. None of the ideas in these essays is difficult. It is possible to talk to students of all ages about the nature of language, learning, thinking, and school. I have given lectures to second graders on psycholinguistics. Primary school children understand ritual—if they are told that is what it is. Teachers will not be able to get rid of programs and testing overnight, but at least they can arm themselves and their students with the understanding that programs and tests are imposed for purposes of control, not to facilitate learning.

How many students ever hear a teacher criticize a course, a book, or a test? How many ever hear a teacher *argue* (as opposed to engaging in a brief one-sided disagreement with them). One change that is essential—and which may provoke the most resistance from individual teachers—is that more than one teacher should be in the classroom for such discussions, even if the class size doubles. Students have no way of learning how to talk with teachers—even if they want to—if they only hear teachers talking to them. Teachers talk differently to students than they talk to each other (just as parents talk differently to babies than to each other—and babies want to learn adult talk, not the way adults talk to babies).

A conventional classroom discussion among teacher and students is nothing like a discussion among teachers in the faculty room—even at the university level. Grade-school teachers can no more say "Go ahead, argue with me" to children than I could say it to my graduate students. Teachers must demonstrate how critical thinking is done; they must initiate students into the club, and to do this they must engage personally in club activities with other members who are prepared and equipped to engage with them.

I would not claim that any of this will change the world overnight. I want to be realistic. But engaging in truly critical thinking in the classroom will give practice not only to students but to teachers as well, and the teacher's aim in the long run must be to educate outside the classroom. Teachers must break the vicious circle that belittles their role and imposes mindless programs on students and teachers alike in the name of education.

The aim must be to construct environments in which critical thinking can take place. The consequence will be revolutionary—but I do not see how we can have critical thinking and maintain the status quo. Any successful attempt to make critical thinking possible for children will lead to radical changes in education. (This is one reason I wonder if all the proponents of critical thinking are really serious.) The mark of the critical thinker is *challenge*, skeptical reflection, suspended assent, the consideration of alternatives. We should not say we want this in our children if we are not prepared to accept it.

On the other hand, change is coming whether we like it or not. Computers are making the conflict between teachers and programs urgent and acute. People who *understand* education must make decisions about how computers are to be used, and the only people who should qualify are teachers and students.

It may be noticed that I have not talked about "methods" at all. Teachers are deceived if they become persuaded that the solution to the critical-thinking issue lies in more exercises, tests and decontextualized activities. These are the problem, not the solution. I have not discussed popular authors who promote instructional packages for developing thinking skills.

The need is not to change children but to change education. How did de Bono and the others learn to think as they do? Not by doing their own exercises. They recommend intellectual games and puzzles that appeal to them—and to the children who can do them—because they have a certain elegance. But the tasks are trivial pursuits, empty pastimes. They do little for children who cannot do them except confirm the belief that the children lack something.

Schools must become places where critical thinking is constant and relevant. I do not see this happening if we continue with educational programming, especially now that so much programmatic instruction can be controlled by computer. The situation is dramatic—in fact it is a cliff-hanger—but realization may be dawning about why education is not working as it should. People are just not thinking enough. By examining why thinking is not more manifest in schools we could unleash an enormously productive and creative intellectual power in both teachers and students.

# Collaboration in the classroom

**5** Collaboration is at the heart of learning in the world outside school. There, children and adults attempt to do something together and the person with more experience helps the novice to succeed. Instead of instruction the beginner receives assistance, which is a much more efficient means of learning than either hypothesis-testing or trial and error. The participation of a more experienced collaborator minimizes mistakes and wasted time. Learners who are helped to achieve a purpose are less likely to be in doubt about what they should do and less likely to acquire irrelevant knowledge and inappropriate behavior.

I shall begin by examining briefly how children obtain essential collaboration in their early learning about spoken language, written language, and the society and culture in which they belong. I shall then consider three vital aspects of collaboration in school—among students, between teachers and students, and among teachers. Collaboration in all these respects is crucial if children are not to be constrained in their opportunities to learn, but such collaboration is difficult to achieve in school situations, especially if there is a constant preoccupation with systematic instruction and tests. When I refer to "schools," incidentally, I use the term generically to include universities. My comments apply to educational institutions at every level, from the primary grades to graduate school.

## Learning outside school

LEARNING SPOKEN LANGUAGE

The role of family and friends in an infant's spoken language development is not complicated; they help the child say what the child is trying to say and they help the child understand what the child is trying to understand. There are no formal periods of instruction in the spoken language club, no curriculum guidelines or objectives, no exercises, and no tests. There are only shared experiences. A child says "Waw waw waw" and an adult says "Please may I have another cookie?" An adult says (in effect) "Quack quack quack" and behaves in a way that a child can understand the utterance to be "Let's go for a walk." Situations that are not made relevant, interesting, or comprehensible to the learner are ignored.

Infants are accepted from birth into a community of spoken language users on the basis of one single criterion—the infants and the more experienced speakers accept each other as the same kind of person. There are no other prerequisites for full participation in mutual activities, and there is never a threat that the newcomer will be rejected for not being as competent as more experienced members of the community. All of the advantages of being a speaker of the language are constantly available to the beginner. The learning is continuous, effortless, and inconspicuous to learner and collaborator alike. George Miller (1977) says that children at this time are "spontaneous apprentices"—they learn from what more experienced people do. In effect, children use more experienced people as unwitting collaborators in their own learning endeavors.

All of this learning takes place with exquisite precision. Children learn to talk precisely like the kind of person they see themselves as being. Children do not practice talking; they *talk*, they listen to what they can understand, and they make very few mistakes. The fact that children are so often right encourages the mistaken view that they cannot be learning very much. The few mistakes they make are regarded as "cute." Only occasionally does someone pause to wonder "Where did the child learn to say that?"

Obviously there can be no formal instruction for learning that is unsuspected by learners and by the people with whom they learn. Obviously such learning cannot be dismissed as "imitation," or "modeling," or "identification" if these terms imply deliberate or organized practice. Children learn without knowing that they are learning—but so do we all. Many adults have been conditioned by the artificial circumstances of formal education to believe that learning is occasional and difficult, requiring effort and deliberate application. In fact learning is normally continual and inconspicuous; we are aware only of failure to learn, of confusion and boredom, just as we are normally more aware of difficulty with breathing than of breathing itself. What is usually called a struggle to learn is actually a struggle to comprehend. When we understand, we learn. The role of the collaborator is to make what is to be learned comprehensible, not by deliberately placing it in a meaningful context but by behaving in a way that is directly relevant to what the learner is trying to accomplish.

## LEARNING TO READ AND WRITE

Long before many children come to school they have been helped to understand a great deal about how written language is used in the community to which they belong (Goelman, Oberg and Smith, 1983). If newspapers are read by their family and friends then children know about newspapers. If catalogs are perused they know about catalogs. If messages are left on refrigerator doors then children know about the kinds of messages that are left on refrigerator doors. They know about television guides and telephone directories, birthday cards, brand names, and traffic signs. Children who are involved in ways of using reading and writing quickly understand such uses and endeavor to use written language in those ways themselves.

Children not only become familiar with the ways in which they see written language being used, they learn about its form. Before children know what a word is they understand that there are spaces in sentences. Long before they know the alphabet they recognize that words consist of letters and have conventional spellings. Once again, little of this learning can be attributed to deliberate instruction. Adults never say to children, "Pay attention in the back there—this is your day for learning about the television guide." Children learn when they are enrolled in the activities of people who use written language, when they join the literacy club. People around them, including other children, help them to read what they are trying to read and to write what they want to write, expanding their horizons all the time.

Mutual engagement in literate activities leads to an even

deeper form of collaboration in which children learn with readers and writers who are not present, who may even be dead. I am referring of course to the authors who show children how written language is produced, helping them to become both readers and writers. But long before children learn through magazines and books in their own hands they have to engage in reading and writing with others who are more proficient.

LEARNING ABOUT THE WORLD

Learning through collaboration is not restricted to language. Children learn to walk like the kind of people they see themselves as being; they learn to dress like them, to groom and ornament themselves like them, and to develop similar interests and values. Children learn about their own society and culture. Little of this learning is a consequence of specific instruction. Instead, more experienced individuals help children to behave in exactly the way that members of their society and culture are expected to behave. They engage in mutual enterprises.

Ask people with specific interests—like writers, musicians, or chess players—how they developed their particular pastimes and occupations, and they are not likely to mention any formal instruction they have received. Instead they will mention a person—who may or may not be a schoolteacher—who was already dedicated to the activity and who introduced the newcomer to it. The more experienced person shared the satisfaction of valued activities. Formal instruction, if it occurs at all, comes later. It can be capitalized upon by those who are already experienced and interested.

Collaboration of this kind is rarely consciously intentional. Situations in which people are mutually engaged make collaboration inevitable as well as inconspicuous. A family member says "There's a big ship," and an infant is helped to recognize ships. A music lover comments on the mellowness of the string section, and a friend learns something about orchestras. Our most important and effective teachers are not those who try to instruct us in what they believe we ought to do, but those who help us to engage in occupations and pastimes they show us are worthwhile. They teach through demonstration and collaboration.

## Collaboration in the classroom

Schools do not facilitate collaboration; they are not places where mutual enterprises are easily undertaken. It could even be argued that schools are designed to interfere with collaboration as much as possible.

Many of the talented people who could recruit children as willing apprentices are excluded from school. I am referring to professional and amateur writers, artists, musicians, athletes, builders, designers, carpenters, sailors, astronomers, gardeners, explorers, ramblers, and the rest; anyone with a *vocation*. Experienced performers and practitioners could demonstrate to children good reasons for engaging in writing, art, music, and so forth, collaborating with children as children strive to engage in such activities themselves. Such "amateurs" are often delighted to have unpaid and informal opportunities to interact with interested children. Unfortunately, potential collaborators are usually only permitted into school outside "teaching" hours, at evenings or weekends, if they are allowed to enter at all.

Ironically, outsiders are excluded because they might interfere with learning. The consequence is an enormous burden upon classroom teachers, who become responsible for all of the learning (and the failure to learn) of their pupils. The teachers also become the sole focus of much of their pupils' frustration and discontent. Yet there is no reason to keep the real world away from the classroom while children get on with the "basics." There is no better way to learn to read and write than to read and write while engaging collaboratively in worthwhile and interesting activities.

There are also walls within schools that inhibit collaboration. The walls of classrooms segregate children on the basis of age and ability as if the ideal were to sort them into identical assemblies of ignorance and incompetence, so that they could never help one another. This is not the way of the world outside school, where older children help younger ones and those who can help those who can't. Halls are expected to be kept empty in schools while children are "learning," except for the congestion of mass transfers from one isolation area to another.

In the following paragraphs I shall discuss reasons why collaboration in school is often so difficult to bring about among students, between students and teachers, and among teachers.

STUDENT-STUDENT COLLABORATION

One of the most unpopular assignments I ever set graduate students in colleges of education was to work together on projects on which they would share the labor and the grade (and the resistance was even greater when I asked them to write papers that would not be graded). The students gave three main reasons why they would prefer not to work together: (1) group work would lead to disputes and lower the quality of the products, (2) somehow all individuals would be trapped into doing more work than their collaborators, and (3) individuals would not get credit for their good ideas, which might in fact be "stolen." In other words, graduate students regarded working in collaboration as less efficient and less rewarding than working alone. Where would anyone learn to look upon collaboration in such a negative way? Where in fact could collaboration be an undesirable activity? The answer, obviously, is in school. Remember, my graduate students were all experienced teachers.

And indeed, I got exactly the same response when second-grade children were encouraged to collaborate on assignments. If the assignment was not to be graded the six-year-olds did not think it worth doing at all, and if it carried a mark they preferred to do it by themselves. Many children (unlike the adults) said that working together was "cheating." Children were so firmly convinced on these points that some of their teachers believed that collaboration was unnatural, and that children were born not wanting to learn unless they could be awarded marks for individual effort. But what the children were in fact demonstrating was exactly what they had been taught in school—that learning is a solitary and competitive matter.

To a large extent, grades and marks are the root of the problem. Grades are the sole reason that most school activities are undertaken, requiring or enticing students to engage in tasks they would never otherwise go near. And grades degrade undertakings that could otherwise be worthwhile in their own right. Make reading newspapers a competitive activity, and readers will be reluctant to share a newspaper with anyone else. Numerical and alphabetic indicators of relative standing do not guarantee good quality work, but working with other people does.

Of course there is "group work" in many classrooms, often termed "collaborative" or "cooperative" learning, but these activities are often arranged for the convenience of the teacher rather than that of the students. The teacher nominates the partners and the tasks, determines when and where the collaboration shall take place, and adds appropriate injunctions about keeping quiet and not making a mess. Children learn, reasonably enough, that the main purpose of the exercise is to enable the teacher to concentrate attention on particular groups and individuals.

It is through mutual endeavors, helping each other, that children (and adults) learn constantly out of school, in their work and their play, so inconspicuously that no one is aware that learning is taking place. Ideally, children of all ages in school should collaborate with each other on what I call *enterprises* (to avoid using otherwise useful terms like "activities" or "projects" that have become hackneyed and distorted in education). Enterprises are group undertakings whose purpose is self-evident. No one who participates in an enterprise ever has to ask, "Why am I doing this?" Examples include the writing of letters (or poems, stories, or articles) that will be produced in conventional form and delivered to appropriate and interested individuals outside the school; designing posters, programs, announcements, and menus for actual use in school or out; building boats, carts, and sheds, planning exhibitions and expeditions, and bringing out a weekly newspaper. The possibilities are endless. Everything that is done with written language outside school can be done within its walls, not as simulations of the "real world" but as authentic activities in their own right.

There are considerable differences between these enterprises and regular school activities. In fact, if activities do not meet four stringent criteria I would not call them enterprises and would not expect them to result in the fluent learning in which all children excel. The first criterion I have foreshadowed: it is *no grades*. Nobody gets "marked" for engaging in any aspect of an enterprise. No one is tested. Enterprises are evaluated, but only in the ways in which all out-of-school enterprises are judged—by their appropriateness, fitness of function, and conformity with standards established by experienced practitioners. Children all recognize that there is a "right" way of doing anything, whether it is dressing for a party, writing a greeting card, or driving an automobile. Children who are doing something for a purpose want to do it in "a proper manner." They will seek correction that helps them to avoid unconventionality or the appearance of ignorance. Children do not need a grade when they are engaged in something they believe is worthwhile. The purpose of the enterprise is the reason for engaging in it and the justification for doing it well.

The second essential criterion for enterprises is *no restrictions*. The world beyond the school walls should not be shut out, nor should enterprises be confined within single classrooms. Children of different ages should do things together, the way they naturally do out of school. Sixth graders are excellent people to read and write with first graders, even if the sixth graders do not read or write very well themselves (in which case the older children benefit particularly from the extra practice). Children take it for granted that they will be helped by older children and should help those who are younger. There is no embarrassment either way, and there is a good deal more understanding and patience than teachers are often able to muster. Older children should not be "teachers" to the younger ones, correcting their work and hearing their catechism, but simply more experienced partners in joint enterprises.

Another kind of restriction to be eliminated is that of the timetable. Enterprises are not started and ended by classroom clocks. Enterprises have their own momentum and their own deadlines—the greeting must arrive before the birthday, the program must be ready for the performance, the magazine has regular publication dates. Any endeavor confined within the restrictions of the classroom becomes just another school activity—a kiss of death almost as lethal as a grade—and loses its meaningfulness as an enterprise. Just one example of the kinds of enterprise that cut across the boundaries of classroom structure and scheduling is the production of plays, operas, or movies, with all their associated writing, planning, casting, rehearsal, performance, business, and promotion. Such ventures occasionally occur as annual events directed by one teacher, but they need not be infrequent or spectacular. There could be much more "off-Broadway." And there could be many more displays, surveys, quests, constructions, and community activities.

The third essential criterion is simply stated: *no coercion*. No one is forced to be part of an enterprise who does not want to be, and no one is excluded because of insufficient talent or experience. Of course, many teachers will object that some children will be reluctant to join enterprises, especially those children who have not had a great deal of success in school activities. How will these children learn if they are not compelled to engage in "learning activities"? But children do not learn when they are bored, confused, or unwilling (except to learn that the compulsory activity is boring, confusing, and to be avoided whenever possible). The role of the teacher is not to force children, which can never result in useful learning, nor to demand that they be interested and attentive when they are obviously bored or bewildered, but to ensure that sufficiently interesting and open enterprises exist to appeal to every child. This is not always easy for teachers, certainly because of the way schools are organized and possibly because of the out-of-school experience of their students. But the "background" of children should never be justification for discarding them in school or for relegating them to monotonous and regimented activities. The more "deprived" the child, the more important the "enriched" environment. Surely the whole point of school is to provide children with opportunities to learn that they would not otherwise be likely to encounter.

The fourth criterion is also difficult for many teachers: *no status*. The distinction between "teachers" and "learners" must be erased. There will always be some members of clubs and participants in enterprises who are more experienced than others, and there may even be management and supervisory functions, but these roles need not be filled by the teacher (and never *because* the person is the teacher). If the teacher is automatically the person in charge, even in pulling strings from offstage, then the activity may again become another school project, engaged in to satisfy or placate authority rather than for intrinsic satisfaction. Teachers must learn to adapt to a different role in school from the one in which many have been inculcated, as the fountainhead of knowledge whose task it is to disseminate wisdom to the minds of ignorant children. This is such an important point that I shall give it a section to itself.

TEACHER-STUDENT COLLABORATION

The most experienced teacher I have ever met had taught at every level from kindergarten to university. She once told me that she had never given a course in which she thought she had nothing to learn. To feel that she already knew everything in advance, she said, interfered both with her teaching and with her students' learning. She saw learning as a mutual enterprise in which teachers might occasionally lead students but never direct them.

Contrast that point of view with the attitude of a distinguished professor when I said I always told students that I expected to learn from them. He was astonished that I should admit that everyone in my classes knew more about some things relevant to the course than anyone else, including the "instructor." "If you tell your students they might know more than you do," my colleague objected, "what defense do you have?"

Some teachers are indeed threatened by the thought that there might be something they do not know; collaboration requires confidence in oneself as well as trust in others. But many teachers also do not see collaboration as their role; they should get on with the job of dispensing "learning." Indeed, a few students in my classes—including some senior administrators—have told me that my responsibility as instructor was to tell them what they were supposed to learn, not to waste time with what they might already know.

But there are many things that teachers do not know. They would not be human if they came into the classroom with no questions about anything. And unfortunately many teachers do not know things they ought to know—like how to be fluent writers. Some teachers try to teach writing although they have never been writers themselves. They have never written a story or poem in their lives, except possibly as a school exercise. Obviously, such teachers should learn to do the things they are hoping to encourage children to do; otherwise the children will simply learn that activities which teachers talk about need not be worth doing in their own right (and that teachers can be hypocritical). Children learn what is demonstrated to them.

Teachers have sometimes told me they intend to become better writers or poets themselves and will take courses in creative writing. I tell them that a much better alternative exists in their own classroom. Teachers should write with their students. When teachers engage in assignments (or better yet, enterprises) with their students, the writing of everyone improves. To learn to write one must read like a writer, which requires behaving like a writer.

Some teachers tell me they could never write poetry or stories with their children. Occasionally teachers think children would feel intimidated by the comparison. More often they confess that their own writing is so poor and unimaginative that they themselves would be embarrassed. Both objections misunderstand the nature of collaboration. When two or more people write collaboratively it makes no sense to talk of who wrote what, just as one cannot analyze who carried which parts when two people together move a heavy box neither could lift alone. In a collaboration, everyone participates and everyone learns. Children also have an important experience when they see a teacher struggling with writing. The popular fallacy that writing is easy for experienced writers is fostered when children see only finished pieces of text. To learn of the frustration as well as the exhilaration of writing, to learn about erasures and abandoned drafts, children need a workshop environment.

Working together with students is certainly the way most teachers will have to learn about computers. Inexperienced teachers cannot expect to learn to use computers intelligently in their classrooms and in their private lives by taking courses on programming and computer literacy. What they need instead is to join a group of people who already use and feel comfortable with computers, and who are willing to share their expertise with beginners. In most schools where there are computers to which students have open access, students are the experts. Even in primary-grade classrooms children who want to know something about a computer tend to go to other children rather than to the teacher. For teachers and children to work collaboratively on mutual enterprises is the ideal way for everyone to learn about computers, as it is to learn about writing.

Experience with computers in classrooms has brought home to many teachers what others have been arguing for years, that teachers must acknowledge that they have to learn with their students. To be an "instructional manager," responsible for the one-way transmission of information to students who have not yet acquired it, is perhaps the greatest impediment that can confront anyone who wants to promote learning. To avoid being burned-out by the stresses of teacher-centered class-rooms and to be an effective guide to all their students, teachers must be learners themselves.

There is a romantic notion that teachers collaborate with students all the time, especially with those students who are having difficulty. The unhappy truth is that "teaching" is often the opposite of collaboration, especially for students who do not do so well. The dispenser of those failing grades is an antagonist.

## TEACHER-TEACHER COLLABORATION

A devastating consequence of the division of schools into cells of twenty, thirty, or more students, all at roughly the same level of ignorance, is that the teacher talks to them in a most peculiar language. This is not an unusual phenomenon. People always speak in odd ways when addressing groups or even individuals with whom they cannot engage in normal conversation. And when all that learners hear is this most peculiar speech being directed at them, they have no opportunity to learn to talk in any normal manner.

Grown-ups, for example, talk to babies in strange ways. They talk to babies in baby talk, and babies are not interested in baby talk. Babies only use baby talk to please adults. Babies are interested in adult language, which they learn only when they hear adults talking to each other. If all that babies hear is adults talking to them, they are deprived of opportunities to learn normal conversation.

A teacher once invited me to observe a classroom "discus-sion," regularly held so that children could talk about each other's writing. Naturally, the teacher expected children to raise their hands to get permission to talk. One child was most anx-ious to say why he liked the story they had read. It was, he said, because the story was "full of detail." The teacher was delighted by the contribution, and quite upset when I suggested that it was nothing like the way anyone normally talks. No one ever urges a friend to see a movie or read a book because it is full of detail (a criterion that would raise telephone directories to the top of the best-seller lists). What the child had learned was classroom talk, the peculiar language of the teacher. The teacher could have helped the students learn how people normally talk about books and films by letting them participate in discussions among the staff.

To learn how teachers really talk, students must hear them talking to each other, an impossibility in a one-teacher classroom. I write from experience. I once complained to a colleague that my own students would never argue with me, even though I gave them every opportunity. I would invite them to state objections and counterarguments to my points of view, and they just sat speechless. My colleague told me why. They had never heard anyone argue with me. "Invite me into your next class," my friend said. "I'll demonstrate how you can be argued with."

I accepted the offer. Within ten minutes my friend and I had a public free-for-all, challenging each other's logic, presuppositions and evidence. We appealed to students to help us make each other see the light, and soon the entire class was arguing with us and with each other. Everyone was learning, including the "instructors," though not in a manner conducive to the quietness expected in educational precincts or to the transmission of predetermined content.

The school day is not designed to facilitate public collaboration among teachers, and many teachers themselves do not like the idea. They are reluctant to share their classrooms with others. They do not encourage visits from other teachers (from the primary grades through graduate school). Even in "team-teaching," individual teachers tend to have particular responsibilities and to talk directly to students rather than to the other members of the team, who indeed may not be present. Yet to reiterate, it is by hearing experienced users of language talking to each other that beginners learn how language is used. Obviously my remarks apply especially to bilingual education and second-language classrooms, where one teacher alone is almost invariably expected somehow to "deliver" the language that students are supposed to learn.

It is not only with language, however, that more than one experienced person is required in learning situations. Learning itself has to be demonstrated. Many of the more general abilities that we strive to develop in children—like inquiry, questioning, problem-solving, inference, critical thinking, and collaboration itself—can only be demonstrated by experienced practitioners interacting with each other. Teachers and their own collaborators must engage in enterprises in which students can join, rather than expecting to organize learning situations among the students themselves.

## Changing schools

I have discussed a variety of ways in which the organization of schools interferes with the development of productive enterprises (with which in fact the structure of the traditional "one-room schoolhouse" was much more compatible). There is not much point in looking to colleges of education to institute improvement by bringing about changes in the way teachers and administrators think. Universities often demonstrate in excess many of the worst teaching practices that I have criticized in schools.

The traditional model of university education could be the ideal for all levels of schooling. I am talking of professors who literally "profess" the *discipline* they follow, who share research and discovery on a tutorial basis with students who are partners in learning enterprises. Colleges of education could be paradigms for collegial learning, with faculty and students alike spending as much time in the classrooms of schools as they do in the classrooms of the university. Instructors and students could strive to understand children and learning together, rather than one group trying to teach "facts" about education to the other. I like one teacher's response to an education professor who proposed an on-site investigation into applications of research in classroom practice. "Fine," said the teacher. "When shall we visit your classroom?"

Tutorials are almost a thing of the past in universities, and when they can be found they are likely to be conducted by assistants rather than by professors. Independent research has been pushed aside by formal course work, or has become an isolated and standardized segment of courses itself. The emphasis is on programs, content, and evaluation. Everything has to be "covered" in one course or another, and instructors are discouraged from straying into areas that are the province of other courses. Everyone is frantically busy but no one has time to talk, to read and to write discursively, or even to think.

If university faculties of education are to be a productive influence on education, they themselves must change through collaboration with schools. Universities most stop regarding themselves as dispensers of wisdom about classrooms, which professors only enter in order to conduct research or to evaluate teachers. Some individual professors and individual teachers are already showing the way, as some always have done, in the mutual enterprise of learning about education, and it is collaboration of this kind that can be a model for changing education in general.

Administrators tend to be suspicious of collaboration in classrooms for the same reasons that it makes many teachers uneasy. Collaborative enterprises look as if they are unorganized, time-consuming, and not necessarily productive. But the real problem, very simply, is that collaboration is *different* from the educational system as it is today. Collaboration is not random behavior; it is not a frill for some at the expense of learning for others. Collaboration works—but it is hard to persuade doubters of the fact by argument. It is similarly difficult to convince the wavering teacher that collaboration is not more demanding of time and skills, and that it does not require more personal attention to individuals. In collaborative enterprises, individuals help each other, and the enterprises become self-sustaining.

Collaboration itself can be a wedge to pry open the rigid structure of formal education. Teachers will not be able to change schools—or the minds of administrators—immediately, but time can always be found for some collaborative enterprises, if only by pushing aside a little formal instruction. Dubious administrators and hesitant teachers are always best persuaded by *results*, and the advantage of collaboration, even though it is radical in terms of the four criteria I cited earlier, is that it demonstrates its own value in terms of interest, productiveness, and learning.

I cannot give further recipes for particular enterprises. Teachers who want to see how writing, for example, can be engaged in collaboratively, should look in the world outside school rather than at videotapes. Editorial offices offer an excellent model. I have been talking about a philosophy, not a method. It is more important to think collaboratively than to try to produce "collaborative behaviors." Many new possibilities will be opened up by computers, provided they are not used in mind-killing iterations of drill and test. Writing, conversation, art, design, and construction can all be engaged in collaboratively by children through computer networks—in which factors like age and size can become irrelevant.

There is one final consideration. When I talk with teachers about the topics of these essays, most of them already know what I am talking about. They do not disagree with me about the desirability of clubs and enterprises, but they find it difficult to bring about the changes they think are desirable. A major problem is lack of support among teachers themselves. Teachers who want to introduce change, even within their own classrooms, face an enormous opposing force of inertia. It is difficult for one teacher, or even one entire school, to change in isolation. Teachers need mutual support, and their own collaborative activities can bring such teachers together.

# The promise and threat of computers in language education

**6** The changes that computers will bring to language, thought, and education are unknown and to a large extent inconceivable. Small computers (also known as personal, home and desktop computers) may do for language and thought what the automobile has done for legs, the jet airplane for jumping. But automobile technology has also produced the tank, and airplanes can carry atomic weapons. Computers have the capacity to devastate literacy and teaching. Teachers cannot barricade their classrooms against computers. But they must not surrender their classrooms either. They must learn what computers can do and how to control them.

It is useless to argue emotionally that computers could never replace teachers. Computers will not go away if we close our eyes to them. More likely they will take over while we are not looking. Many influential people, including computer and educational programmers, software developers, politicians, and administrators, believe that computers can teach anything that is expected of them. They believe that computers are cheaper than teachers, which is true—for those things that computers are able to teach. They also believe that computers are more efficient than teachers, which is also true—to the same limited extent. The question is not whether computers should be allowed in classrooms but how they are to be used. More precisely, the question is who is to be in charge. To understand these issues, we must consider what computers can do.

## Uses of computers

The uses of computers can be categorized in many arbitrary ways. I shall focus on five of their most visible contemporary functions, as (1) game-playing devices, (2) information sources, (3) teachinig machines, (4) creative tools, and (5) communication links. Most of my opening comments will focus on negative aspects of computers, but I shall end on a more optimistic note.

## GAME-PLAYING DEVICES

I mention game playing first because computers are currently so conspicuous in this way. From an educational point of view I regard this recreational utility as indisputable but irrelevant. There is nothing wrong with playing games on computers, but it is not their most enlightened or productive function for language learning. Games can be a powerful incentive to get children to concentrate on less interesting activities, but any drill or exercise that requires an irrelevant reward for a student to attend to it is an exercise or drill that is a waste of time in any case. To learn about language, children need experience in language. Such experience may be introduced to a child through computer games, but it is a roundabout way of proceeding. Language is predominantly the concern of people, not of machines. There are many direct ways for children to gain familiarity with a new language, written or spoken, and I shall enumerate some in a later section. Many of these alternatives can involve computers, but always in an immediate and practical way, not as a consolation or reward for boring and pointless exercises.

The increasing use of computer "simulations" of real life states of affairs is one aspect of game playing that may have some important educational implications. With a computer one can practice landing a jet airplane without jeopardizing life or equipment, and so realistically that even professional pilots are trained in this way. In such simulations, of course, a few specialized aspects of language may be learned, like the jargon of air crew and of air traffic controllers. It is tempting to believe that simulations could provide rich opportunities for language learning and practice generally, but I do not see any great necessity or advantage in this. Learners can be put directly in touch with language users and language use for many valid and self-evident reasons, with or without the use of computers, and without the need for simulation. Games and simulations may be visible and attractive uses for computers, but so is the fact that you can put a flowerpot on the console. The most obvious use is not necessarily the most relevant for language instruction.

INFORMATION SYSTEMS

I am similarly neutral about the educational potential of computers as information management systems. Computers already constitute enormous resources for the acquisition, organization, storage, and retrieval of information. Banks, insurance companies, airlines, hospitals, universities, government itself—none of our large institutions and few commercial enterprises could survive today without computers. Our lives depend on them, though we may not know it. But I do not see computers taking the place of libraries, film, or people in providing experience rather than information. And experience rather than information is the essence of language learning. Instead, computers can facilitate access to possibilities of experience through relevant books, films, and people. If I want to call a particular telephone number it will be easier to have a computer look it up and dial it for me than to do all this myself. But if I want the experience of talking with the person at that number, then I will not leave everything to the computer. If I want to read a particular book, the most I want the computer to do is locate the book for me—at least until the time that a computer is as portable and as aesthetically pleasing as a book. And if I am interested, say, in experiencing life in a particular part of the world, an actual visit or a film will still be a preferable alternative to inspecting the statistics or learning the facts that a computer could present to me.

Two aspects of the information-managing capabilities of computers that many professional writers have found invaluable are those of checking spelling and suggesting vocabulary. No need to worry about the spelling of those awkward words—just put down anything, an initial letter even, and sort it all out with the computer's own spelling list when the composition is done. No need to go to the thesaurus for the word that is on the tip of your tongue—a touch of a key will provide you with a set of synonyms (or antonyms) for any notion you have in mind.

Teachers may well object to these time-, labor- and attention-saving facilities that computers offer for the same reason that there have been objections to typewriters and pocket calculators in classrooms, that they may make learning basic skills unnecessary and therefore interfere with learning. Such teachers mistakenly believe that obstacles are efficacious motivators. But there is no evidence that making an activity difficult facilitates learning. Quite the reverse; difficulty with spelling and vocabulary inhibits writing. Learners try to avoid those words that might be wrong, and in the long run the difficulty interferes with learning about written language. A comfortable facility with reading and writing (and with mathematics), on the other hand, makes the continual learning of the "basics" both effortless and natural.

Problems arise with computers as information management systems when "facts" and "data" that may be stored in them are mindlessly dumped on children to be learned by rote. A computer always ready to generate the desired tense of any regular or irregular verb on request could be a boon to any learner. The same computer used as a mechanical taskmaster to drill or test a child on those same conjugations according to someone else's prescription changes a useful facility to a meaningless ritual.

DRILL MACHINES

It is as drill-and-test devices—sometimes euphemistically referred to as teaching machines—that computers today are widely seen as most relevant to education. And it is as such devices that computers are potentially most dangerous. Not only are they capable of presenting the most trivial, decontextualized, and fragmented drills in endless variation, they do so extremely efficiently and in a manner highly attractive to both students and teachers. They are compelling in their authority. Perhaps the biggest risk lies in their power to persuade that they are worth attention.

Uncertain or apprehensive teachers are generally content to hand over the task of constructing programs to experienced software producers. But the repetitive presentation of simple questions, with responses checked against "correct" answers and results scored and stored for future reference, is in fact among the easiest kind of computer program to write. Every bit of nonsense drill ever put on paper can be reproduced in computer software, and in living color as well, by "experts" with little or no educational or linguistic competence.

Educators themselves do not necessarily demonstrate greater sophistication, however. At several recent educational conferences I have heard linguists, teachers, and other specialists in language education discuss how computer software might be developed for second-language instruction. Most of the time they talked in terms of what they thought the computer could most conveniently do. They talked of repetitive tasks with right and wrong answers, the correction of errors, of tests, scores, and the keeping of records, the grist of mechanical programmed instruction, all totally unrelated to the way language is naturally learned and used. They talked frequently and even cheerfully about language that would be distorted in some way, of sentences and paragraphs containing blanks for the student to complete, or containing extraneous words for the student to remove, and even of totally nonsensical random arrangements of words that the computer would obligingly generate for the student to reorganize. All of this was highly ingenious in conception and application, and all of it was totally unnatural. Whatever these experts were talking about, it was not language as it could conceivably be employed among real people. No one in real life ever leaves blanks in speech for the listener to complete or adds extraneous words for the listener to detect and eliminate. Parents do not speak nonsense to children, which is just as well because children might then get the idea that language was nonsensical, a notion that some producers of language instruction programs could be thought to be trying to inculcate deliberately. I do not think the experts in the software workshops at language education conferences wanted to convey to learners that language could be totally meaningless. But they were not using their understanding of learners or language at all—they were thinking of what the computer could do, distorting language to accommodate what they perceived to be the possibilities and limitations of the computer.

For anyone who thinks that language learning will take place only if it is continually monitored and measured, preferably in predetermined small quantities, or who believes that anything a drill can teach must be important, especially if it is packaged and promoted under the label of some important-sounding skill, then computer-based instruction is enormously attractive. It is not difficult to impress unsuspecting teachers with such programs and to get children to attend to them. Any kind of nonsense can be made more palatable for children if presented in a "game" atmosphere—just as it is not difficult to persuade them to prefer junk food to nourishment. This is truly seduction of the innocent, accomplished by an occasional happy face, ten minutes of Pac-man, and, if necessary, the blandishments of a misguided teacher. One large educational software company currently boasts in its advertising that it can get children to attend to "learning" activities that would be too boring if presented in any other way. What will such programs really teach children about language?

"Drill and kill" can fatally damage both literacy and teaching. To anyone who holds that the development of language ability is a matter of rote learning the basic skills through systematic instruction—and unfortunately there seem to be well-meaning people who have that belief—computers can not only do the job of language teachers, they can do it better. Computers can lead us faster all the way down the path to totally controlled programmatic language instruction. This is not mere doomsaying. I am not talking about a possible world of tomorrow. In Britain today there is already in operation a system called *telesoftware downloading*. In a growing number of classrooms, the British Broadcasting Corporation has its own computer, the cheap and highly adaptable Acorn, which the teacher at the end of classes every day can leave plugged into the national television system. During the night, when there is no television broadcasting, software for the next day's instruction is "downloaded" into all of the BBC computers, ready for the teacher next morning. The only reasons the system has not so far had a more dramatic effect on British education are that not every classroom has its own computer and not enough software exists. Both handicaps are receiving immediate attention, however. How long will it be, one wonders, before it is realized that such a fully operational system does not need teachers or classrooms?

THE CREATIVE ALTERNATIVE

If my approach to computers in language education has so far seemed cautious, if not antipathetic, it is because I wanted to consider the dangers first. They are the most immediate. More is known about the risks than about the constructive possibilities, which is one reason so many people think that computers should be kept out of classrooms. Nevertheless I think every schoolchild should have easy access to computers, especially the youngest, especially in language education, because of two other aspects of computer use I have yet to mention, their two most positive and favorable possibilities.

Consider how the computer as a creative tool can help authors. For a start, it will take care of two of the greatest concerns of beginning writers and of all fluent writers—legibility and speed. Readability is always a problem for authors, even if not at the fetish level that neatness often becomes in classrooms. One touch of a computer keyboard and you have a perfectly formed letter that can be printed in a compact and properly aligned orientation. No need even to remember that in English print goes from left to right, from top to bottom. Typewriters offer the same advantages, of course, but at the cost of flexibility. It is difficult to erase or to write something between the lines with a typewriter and impossible to work vertically, to move text or to draw arrows connecting one part with another. But the word processor combines the speed and ease of the most sensitive electric typewriter with the maneuverability of a pencil on paper. Transferring words, sentences, or paragraphs from one place to another is a simple matter on the word processor, and always the result is clean and legible; no need for the continual, tedious, and time-wasting rewriting of drafts. Trying something out to see how it looks is easy, and so is recovering what you had before. Working on two or more things at the same time is easy. This is *control*, power in the service of creativity, something that all children understand, that their language and brains inevitably seek. Word processors make writing a plastic art.

I have not been talking about the value of word processors for experienced authors, or even for experienced secretaries. My concern has been with what computers can do to help individuals in difficulty, whether an author struggling with ideas on the fringe of formation and expression, a secretary attempting to organize a text neatly, efficiently, and fast, or a learner overburdened with both the author's and the secretary's concerns—and striving to learn more about language as well. I have also not just been talking about the production of books, but about all of the activities that can and should provide opportunities for learning in any language classroom, everything that can be written, read, and talked about, like letters, labels, lists, notes, memoranda, newspapers, magazines, reviews, digests, programs, advertisements, plans, schedules, recipes, and timetables, all part of the very fabric of a living language.

But few people have even begun to explore the power and potential that computers offer language. To get even a feel of the future we do better to look at two other creative fields, music and art. In music, for a few hundred dollars, you can get a keyboard to connect to your computer. Play three notes and the computer will remember them for you and play them again, as often as you wish. You would rather try three different notes? The computer will remember and play them. You prefer the first three? Touch a key and they are retrieved. You would like to hear the six together? Repeatedly? In reverse order? Twice as fast? Transposed up or down a tone? In waltz time? Syncopated? Counterpointed? Harmonized? With percussion? On the brass? Bring in the woodwinds? The ever-patient computer will do it all at the beckoning of a fingertip. And when you have all the parts of your concerto together you can perform it on your digital stereo, make any last changes you wish, and finally command the computer to print out the score for you. You can compose, conduct, and revise your own composition as often as you like. None of the great classical composers could do any of that. That is the power the computer offers to music.

For another few hundred dollars you can buy a graphics tablet—or perhaps a different computer—to see what the computer will do for art. You draw a squiggle with a "pen" and the squiggle appears on the screen. Touch a key and the squiggle is erased. Touch another and it returns. Work the squiggle into a tree and the computer will save it for you. You would like a cow to go under the tree? The computer will find for you the one you drew yesterday. You prefer the rather compelling cow that I drew? The computer will get it. The cow is too large? Touch a key and you change its size. It is facing the wrong way? Touch a key and it turns around. You want a family of cows in descending order of size? In different colors? You want them to *move*? You can't draw straight lines? Circles defeat you? None of these fazes the computer. It will even put a frame around the picture for you. No need to wait for the paint to dry before you can see how it would look in different tones, or in a different size, reversed, or in a different kind of frame. The touch of a few keys will change the scene from dawn to dusk, from summer to winter. All this is *power* once again— power to develop and fulfill the driving, creative impulses of the human brain. One does not have to instruct a child in the desirability of such power. Rather, adults must learn from children. I have seen artwork produced on computers by six-year-olds that is equaled in originality and imaginativeness only by those principal commercial manifestations of computer art, record covers, rock videos, and television advertisements.

What will the computer do for language and thought? I can only offer another analogy. I heard recently of young quadri-plegics, of victims of cerebral palsy, regarded even by their helpers almost as vegetables because of their inability to control movement, to communicate, or to express themselves. They were provided with computerized keyboards consisting of a small number of symbols, which they could activate in some way—poking at them with a toe, an elbow, or with a "unicorn's horn" strapped to the forehead. The technology exists today to activate a key simply with a glance, almost by an act of will, the way an artificial limb can be controlled by a muscle twitch. With the way opened for these mute youngsters to enter the world of language they quickly exhausted the possibilities of the keyboard, demanded hundreds and even thousands of new symbols, invented their own meaningful combinations, and spent hours of their days and nights talking to each other. One of the staff described how suddenly she realized that inside each one of these clumsy, limited, inarticulate adolescents was a lively, intelligent, creative, language-using individual—waiting to be released.

Here is a sobering thought. We are *all* physically handicapped. Within the limitations of our clumsy bodies, of our sluggish sensory and perceptual processes, of the lumbering rate at which we are all able to speak, write, and draw, there is an inconceivably more lively, intelligent, and creative individual waiting to be released. What will computers do for language and thought?

How can we learn about the possibilities of computers? In what directions should we proceed? There is no point in asking any adult in the world today. We all grew up in the B.C. era—before computers. Computers constitute a new culture. To live with them requires a new language. To understand them demands individuals without fear or preconceptions who can rapidly learn to make sense of a new language and to feel quickly at home in a new culture. Fortunately such individuals exist in large numbers in every generation. I am referring of course to children. The time has come in education when we must at last acknowledge that the greatest source of learning for teachers must be children.

## COMPUTERS AND COLLABORATION

A misconception prevails that computers are solitary devices that isolate their users from the real world and particularly from other people. Nothing is further from the case. Computers can dissolve the walls of classrooms, collapse space as well as time, and bring people together in dramatic new ways.

In writing, for example, two people can undertake joint authorship far more easily than they can with typewriters or even pencils and paper. No need for a collaborator to lean over a child's shoulder any more. No need to take something from someone in order to read it. I can show you what I am writing simply by reproducing my screen on your screen with a touch of a key. I can disclose to you all the contents of my memory (in computer terms, at least). You can comment on what I have written, even suggest alterations, while on my screen I observe what you do, as you do it. If your changes please me I can accept them, and if they do not my original text will not be affected.

For two people to be able to write together in this direct, collaborative way is to my mind the most dramatic development in writing technology since it became possible for individuals to write at all. And the collaborative technology exists today in many forms—though its possibilities are widely misunderstood. For example, one networking system designed for school use has a key that can be touched so that what is on the screen or in the memory of any computer in the room can be inspected. A second key permits changes to be made on any screen. And a third key, an override, can be used to prevent anyone else actually inspecting or changing what you have produced without your consent. Marvelous possibilities for collaboration— except that in the system I have described, only the teacher has the three keys.

In second-language instruction in Canada, many children in English-speaking regions are laboriously drilled in French in the fond hope that one day they might be able to write a letter to a child in a French-speaking community. But already the technology exists for a child in Vancouver and a child in Quebec City to write a letter *together*, collaborating on the text more closely than if they were sitting side by side with pencils and paper. Already, children in Fairbanks, Alaska, and in Frobisher Bay are conversing directly by computer.

We can all be closer in the future through computers. Readers will be closer to authors, writers to editors, learners to practitioners. I may not have to wait for my favorite author's next novel to be published. If the author agrees, I will be able to read it as it is being written, making the author my collaborator as I vicariously write the story, sharing the excitement and frustration of composition and the discipline of revision and editing.

### The role of teachers

Of course there will still be a role for teachers, the same club role that I have argued is the critical one for language teachers in any case. Teachers must demonstrate to children what language—and computers—might be used for and help children to be users themselves. The teacher's role will not be to instruct the child but to collaborate in activities that are mutually interesting and rewarding. Both teacher and student learn because they share the same objectives, because they are members of the same language-users' club, or community, even if their abilities differ.

Computers offer marvelous possibilities in language education still largely unexplored, but they must be used intelligently. Teachers, not computers, must be in charge of what goes on in the name of language education, which means that teachers must understand computers and not be afraid of them. They are no more threatening than pianos.

The fundamental rules for computer use in language education are not complicated. Computers should not be used to engage learners in nonsensical, pointless, or painful activities, and they should not be allowed to determine what learners and teachers do next. They should not be permitted to trivialize or distort language. They should not be expected to take charge of language education, which will still basically require people as models and as collaborators. Computers should be exploited as a powerful means to facilitate access to language and the use of language.

Teachers themselves must learn about computers. Fortunately, every teacher with access to a computer has an opportunity to do this, not by rushing off and taking the nearest course in computer literacy, uselessly wrestling with the history of computers and the logic of Boolean algebra, but by taking the opportunity to learn *with* children. In most schools where computers are freely available to students today, students are the experts. Rigorous, time-consuming, programmatic instruction is not required to teach children to understand computers. They need only unshackled opportunity to learn—and they can demonstrate their understanding to teachers. As I have already said, with computers all teachers must be ready finally to acknowledge that education is a reciprocal activity, that the true teacher learns with the students.

All this has been about the short run, about the next ten years, perhaps. For the more distant future I think no one can tell. Computers may not make schools totally unnecessary (though they might) but they will certainly change their character. They will dissolve the walls that for better or worse have for so long separated schools from the world outside. But the basic issue for language instruction will remain unchanged from what it is today, indeed from what it was before computers began to make that basic issue more acute and critical. That issue is the fundamental one of how language should be taught, by rote and exercise or by demonstration and engagement.

My concern has not been about narrow theoretical questions. The matters to which I have addressed myself are not fundamentally philosophical, pedagogical, or even practical. The issue is essentially political. I have been talking about control.

The question that must now be confronted is who will make the decisions that determine how children learn, teachers working directly and collaboratively with children, or "programmers" pulling the strings from outside? If teachers and children are able to make use of the creative and interactive potential of computers, then I believe we are on the threshold of a world of learning scarcely imaginable. The alternative is the employment of computers in ways that will destroy literacy and teachers. And teachers alone must decide and assert how computers will be used in education.

# Misleading metaphors of education

Language is transparent. We look through the words and perceive the meaning, just as we look through a window and see the view. We cannot see the words and the meaning at the same time any more than we can simultaneously inspect the view and the glass in the window.

Sometimes a window is opaque. There are blemishes on the surface and we become more aware of the glass than of what we are trying to see. In the same way, individual words may divert our attention as we listen or read, so that awareness of the words comes between us and the meaning. Like poorly constructed glass, inadequate words obscure the scene beyond.

Sometimes particular kinds of refracting glass can be employed to enhance the way we see; they are windows that augment vision. Periscopes, microscopes, and telescopes enable us to look round corners, magnify parts of objects or bring them closer to us. But sometimes such a glass can distort perception, like the fish-eye lens of the camera, the convex glass of the makeup and shaving mirror, or the undulating reflectors of the fairground. The reality of what we see in these circumstances is often compelling. Nothing in the perception itself tells us that the world is being distorted. Unless we *know* that what we see is not really what we are looking at, we believe what we perceive and do not even suspect that we are being misled.

Language is transparent . . . I am speaking metaphorically, of course. Metaphors are the refracting lenses of language. Sometimes they help us to perceive a meaning more clearly —as I hope the metaphor of transparency is doing now. But sometimes metaphors distort our understanding; they make us perceive and think in ways that are inappropriate. And the fact

that they do so may not even be suspected. The most misleading metaphors are those that we do not think are metaphors
at all.

In this essay, I shall examine five metaphors widely used in
literacy education. They are so common in discussions of reading, writing, and teaching that it is often not realized that they
are metaphors. We look right through them and perceive what
we are thinking or talking about differently from the way the
world really is.

The five metaphors to which I refer are *information, process,
skills, levels* and *stages*. At first glance they may appear to be
unobjectionable words, crystal-clear even. But they can be as
delusory as bottle-glass. In the following pages I shall look at
each of the five in turn, considering first the metaphorical ways
in which the word is used, then the inappropriateness and
dangers of these uses. I am not conducting a campaign to stamp
out metaphors; that would be absurd. It would not be easy
even to replace the five that are my particular concern. But I
shall suggest how we might protect ourselves from their more
unfortunate distortions.

## Information

I begin with a word I once used extensively myself, so I must
temper my criticism when other people do the same. But we
can be just as misled by the words we use ourselves as by the
words of others, and our own language is always a good place
to begin an analysis of this kind. The word *information* must
be one of the most popular and least scrutinized words in
education today. I especially want to examine how the word
is used in references to literacy in particular and to learning in
general. The fact that the same expressions can make themselves at home in such diverse environments should raise doubts
about their validity. Reading, for example, is often "defined"
or referred to as the acquisition of information, and so are
learning and education. Writing is seen as the transmission of
information from one person to others, and so is teaching. The
brain itself can be described as an information-processing device, and thinking as information processing. The jargon is so
pervasive that few people, especially those who use it most,

stop to ask what is really being talked about, and whether the language is appropriate.

READING AND WRITING

What is wrong with thinking that reading is the acquisition of information? It is, isn't it? Don't we get information every time we read? What is the point of reading if no information is acquired?

For a start, we do not realize that we are talking in a very peculiar way. "Getting information" is not the reason we do most things in life. We don't say that we are going for a walk to acquire information, that we want to see a movie for information, that we plan to phone home and exchange a lot of information, or even that we are reading a novel for information. A telephone directory, perhaps, but a novel? It is possible to strain the language and to assert that all these events "really are" the acquisition of information, just as a few people have even tried to tell me that listening to music is a matter of acquiring information, but to do so simply perverts the normal use of a perfectly good word and makes it meaningless. If everything is going to be called information, then the word differentiates nothing and a new word will have to be found for that which really *is* information, which I (and the dictionary) take to be anything that enables us to make a decision for a specific purpose. There is an alternative word, *experience*, which refers to the fundamental concerns of living and learning, and which seems to me to be a better description and justification of the kinds of activity I have just listed—including most of our reading. The danger in using the word *information* with such abandon is simply that we believe what we say; we take the word literally. We take it for granted that reading is a matter of acquiring information—and behave and teach accordingly.

Louise Rosenblatt (1978) distinguishes two kinds of reading, which she calls *efferent* and *aesthetic*. Efferent reading is reading that is indeed done for the sake of information, like looking something up in a telephone directory, a catalog, a television guide, or a textbook. Efferent reading is easy to recognize— you want to finish it as quickly as possible and would be quite happy to get the information in some other way (by being told, for example). Aesthetic reading, on the other hand, is reading engaged in for the pleasure of the activity, like reading a novel or poem (or in certain circumstances a newspaper or magazine). With aesthetic reading we do not want other people to save us the trouble by telling us what is going to happen. We may even slow down as we near the end so that we can extend the satisfaction we are getting. Aesthetic reading, in other words, is done for experience, not for information. Experience may provide information as a by-product, but information can never provide experience. And experience, I shall argue, is the basis of learning.

The classroom tragedy, says Rosenblatt, is that reading that should be aesthetic is transformed into the efferent variety. She satirizes the situation in an article with the sardonic title: " 'What facts does this poem teach you?' " (Rosenblatt, 1980). Why should pleasurable aesthetic experience be distorted into miserable information-acquisition activity? There can be only one explanation: to give a grade. How can a person's reading pleasure or satisfaction be evaluated objectively? How can experience be scored as correct or incorrect? Reading is distorted to focus on an aspect that can be controlled and counted, and then it is assumed that the aspect that is isolated is the most essential. To look upon information acquisition as the sole or even the most important function of reading is to employ an inappropriate image. It is like looking at reading through a microscope or the wrong end of a telescope. A detail is magnified and assumed to be the whole.

Writing suffers in the same way. Two of the most valuable and satisfying uses of writing are the creation and sharing of experience with other people and the exploration of ideas, not the transmission of information. Often we write about what our readers already know, just as interesting conversations can be recapitulations or extensions of experiences we have shared, like talking about a movie we saw together. I do not expect or intend to *transmit information* to readers in this essay, but rather to construct a landscape of ideas that we can jointly explore. Conclusions that readers might draw from what I write are less likely to be based on information I have provided than on insights and understanding they bring themselves. I probably get as much from anything I write as any reader. In fact, one of the most important functions of writing is largely concealed from children in school (and from university students), namely, writing to explore one's own ideas and to generate new ones. The most productive writing that we all do may be writing that no one else ever sees—hardly writing that falls into the "information-transmission" category. And it may be this genre of expressive, personal writing that motivates children to become writers in the first place, not writing for other people (who in a child's experience can be very picky and discouraging about anything shown to them).

The problem with the information-transmission perspective in writing instruction is that it invariably takes the point of view of a mythical reader. A child may write about a fascinating imagined event, recreate an important personal experience, or express an exciting or disturbing idea or feeling, even if it is only sketched out in what to others are a few inadequate words. The young author might indeed like to show this creative production to a considerate adult, the way we all like to share the achievements that please and impress us. But if the adult, teacher, or parent, responds with negative comments about spelling, neatness, and the brevity of the piece, then the adult is treating the child's writing in terms of information transmitted, not experience shared. What is the effect on the *writer?* Writing in order to convey information has utility, but it is not the most compelling reason for children to learn to write. They do not have a lot of information to convey—and it may seem to them that the only reason many people want information at all is to evaluate the transmitter.

How should reading and writing be perceived, if the information-transmission metaphor is inappropriate? There cannot be just one metaphor, just as there cannot be one definition; reading and writing fulfill a range of purposes that I think can extend across all human endeavor. But if just one aspect of reading and writing must be highlighted then perhaps it should be *the creation and sharing of experience*—the generation of possibilities of knowing and feeling. Authors create landscapes of ideas and experience through which they and their readers may travel and explore. Reading and writing are creative enterprises, not the shunting of information.

LEARNING AND TEACHING

The idea that learning is a matter of acquiring information, which it is the job of teachers to transmit, fits well into the contemporary production-line model in which schools "deliver instruction" to students.

The production-line approach, which I call *programmatic instruction*, is based on the mistaken notion that a child can be taught any subject, and taught how to read and write, one systematic bit at a time, especially if there are frequent tests. Teach a child everything an expert knows, and you will finish up with another expert. Such a view completely ignores why experts learned what they know and the circumstances in which they learned it. Fact learning is not the basis of most abilities; it is a consequence. Knowledge of the sounds of letters does not make children readers any more than knowledge of dates makes historians. Becoming readers and writers enables children to master the "basics" or the "mechanics," not vice versa. Delivering specific information in systematic ways is more a matter of control than of teaching, designed to facilitate the evaluation of teachers and students alike at the cost of fragmenting, decontextualizing and trivializing what is to be learned.

The consequence of the view that learning is the acquisition of facts is perhaps most conspicuous at universities. Even graduate students are persuaded—and often rightly so—that the main objective in a course is to get high grades by feeding back the "facts" the instructor has given, or that are found in books students have been told to read. What is the value of exploring other points of view if they will not be questioned on them, or given credit for their own ideas? The essential part of the transaction is the *course content*, the information the instructor dumps on the student and which the student in turn is supposed to demonstrate having acquired by dumping it back on the instructor. The procedure is dignified with the name of "scholarship." And all of this begins in grade school, where "research" becomes a matter of showing that you have discovered what the teacher expects you to find out—some "facts" that can be marked right or wrong.

AN ALTERNATIVE PERSPECTIVE

Learning is not a matter of stuffing your head with information, of becoming a walking compendium of facts. Learning is complex and subtle, with a variety of characteristics including (to mention a few that are conspicuously different from information-acquisition) imagination, hypothesis-testing, discrimination, estimation, purpose, and reflection. None of these is a separate stage or skill that can be taught in isolation. All must be involved in even the simplest gathering of facts; otherwise information acquisition is pointless as well as difficult. Information acquisition is the hard way to become an idiot savant. Learning is creative, inseparable from experience (the very word has the same root as "experiment"), and teaching has to be the provision of experience from which the desired learning can creatively take place.

Rather than demonstrating how much more there is to learning and to living than mere information-processing, however, cognitive psychology has gone the other way and accepted the information-processing metaphor as its own. The brain is seen as an information-processing device. A popular introductory psychology text is entitled *Human Information Processing* (Lindsay and Norman, 1977). But as I have pointed out in the final chapter of *Essays into Literacy* (Smith, 1983), the brain does much more than store information, and it is not even particularly good at acquiring and storing information. The brain is not a telephone switchboard, or a library, or even a computer. I cannot say what the brain *is*, in any literal sense, but I know what it is like. The brain is like an artist. It learns creatively, and anything that stultifies its creativity interferes with learning. By employing a dull and inappropriate metaphor, we perceive learning and try to promote it in dull and inappropriate ways.

## Process

The image of the brain as a device that operates upon information leads almost inevitably to the notion that it functions by engaging in various kinds of *process*. Just as there are specialized industrial processes for the production of everything from paper clips to aircraft carriers, so the brain is seen as engaging in processes for the production of writing, reading, comprehension, and even thought. The word *process* has become ubiquitous, especially in professional and research journals. One rarely sees the word *reading* alone, but only as part of "the reading process." Writing has become "the writing process." Learning is "the learning process" and thinking "the thinking process." The reading process comprises decoding and comprehension processes, writing has drafting and editing processes, and so on, ad infinitum.

This rash of processes may seem impressive at first glance, as if everything is being brought under control, which I suppose is the main reason the word is used, even if unconsciously. But to call something a process usually adds nothing. One could go through most of these texts deleting the word (and its attendant article) without making the slightest difference, except for reducing the risk of inappropriate thought. To talk about teaching the writing process, for example, rather than simply about teaching writing, lends itself easily to the production-line model of breaking things down into parts and teaching them one meaningless bit at a time.

I can give a specific illustration. Two insightful researchers at the University of New Hampshire, Donald Murray and Donald Graves, did a service to children by pointing out to their teachers that professional writers rarely expect their own efforts to be successful the first time. Authors usually work on several drafts before they are satisfied, and they are not too fussy at these times about spelling, complete sentences, or neatness, leaving such matters aside until they are revising and editing. Drafting and editing might be considered as different *aspects* of writing that experienced writers usually engage in as they go along, drafting when they get or need ideas for the future, and editing when they are reviewing what they have written so far.

But what are simply aspects of writing when we talk about it in a normal way become stages or components when writing is perceived as a process. Suddenly everything becomes sequential and separable, with drafting and editing seen as subprocesses, or processes in their own right, that can be taught and learned independently of any more meaningful aspects of writing. Writing becomes part of a sequence that begins with prewriting and ends with rewriting (sometimes labeled more poetically as prevision, vision, and revision). Educational publishers have produced posters, which no doubt finish up on classroom walls, with the following breakdown: "THE WRIT-ING PROCESS: (1) prewriting (2) writing (3) rewriting." And of course there are kits of materials for each of these activities. All of this is a travesty of the original intention. Yet two teachers proudly told me once that in their schools they were doing exactly what Graves recommended—their children were pre-writing on Mondays and Tuesdays, writing on Wednesdays, and rewriting on Thursdays and Fridays.

Not all teachers are as literal as those I have just mentioned, but the example illustrates the dangers of calling a global en-terprise, like writing, a process. The metaphor stretches it out, breaks it up into parts, and makes it particularly susceptible to programmatic instruction, removing all the sense from what is to be learned and making learning difficult if not impossible.

The problem has been around with reading for many years, the metaphor of processes now replacing the earlier term "subskills"—like letter-identification, sound-blending and sight-word recognition—for what has to be mastered before anything meaningful about reading can be attempted or even encoun-tered. And the image is rapidly generating materials and tests in new areas, such as the listening process and a host of critical thinking processes. A good metaphor goes a long way.

The brain does not consist of processes nor does it learn by acquiring them. We may *know of* processes—like how a ce-ramic pot is made, or a radio put together, or steel smelted, but these are sequences of physical or technological operations that have no literal counterpart in the mental condition of the brain. Our feet are involved in a pedaling motion when we ride a bicycle, but no part of the brain engages in such rotary move-ment. Reading, writing, and thinking are conditions or situations with many inseparable aspects, primarily constructive and cre-ative.

Finally, the notion that the brain consists of specialized pro-cesses further supports the view, already widely established, that every aspect of our mental lives is a skill. This leads to my next quarry.

## Skills

*Skills* is another word so frequently used that teachers are rarely aware of the connotations it may have, the excess baggage it can bring with it. Like the cuckoo that pushes the rightful but less aggressive tenants from the nest, so *skills* has taken over from more neutral words like *ability*.

Many people rarely talk any longer about learning to read, and it is unusual to see such a meat-and-potatoes expression in print. If the topic is not "learning the reading process" then it will be "learning (or acquiring) reading skills." Or writing skills, or thinking skills. The word is used so extensively that it is taken for granted, as if it had always been around. Surely reading and writing are skills; or involve skill. Well, *skill* and *skills* have been in use in the English language for a long time, but not in connection with mental activities like reading and writing. Their general use in connection with literacy is a phenomenon of the 1950s and 1960s, when the massive promotion of programmatic instruction began and everyone had to become objective and specific, or at least to talk in that way. Earlier, anyone who wanted to talk about how well a child could read or write (and who was not content simply to talk about good or poor readers and writers), talked of reading and writing "ability." Now, however, the talk is always about skills. The tests always examine skills. Publishers produce skills kits and materials. And teachers are expected to conform to objectives specified in terms of skills, and even to compose such objectives themselves.

So what difference does it make if we talk about skills rather than ability? Isn't this just playing with words? The difference may be profound, because of the images and associations each word conjures up in our minds, even without our consciously thinking about it. *Skill* and *ability* are not synonymous. It is a matter of what we take for granted.

Traditionally, and I suspect in the out-of-school lives of most individuals as well, the word *skill* is employed with respect to physical activities, either sporting (the skills of rowing or high-jumping) or manual (the skills of carpentry or embroidery). The distinctive characteristic of all these activities is that they involve physical dexterity, or motor coordination, and frequently muscular strength as well. And it seems to me (though I am told it is not necessarily the case) that both motor coordination and muscular strength increase with exercise, drill, and practice.

But cognitive abilities like reading, writing, and thinking are not the kinds of activities that improve with exercise and drill.

The brain has no muscles to strengthen through repetitive activities, and no motor coordination is involved (except for physical concomitants like handwriting). When we talk about reading and writing skills we are speaking metaphorically, and the metaphor can be inappropriate. Literacy is not developed through practice and drill.

This is not to say that children need not engage in reading and writing. They should read and write, much more than most of them do at present. But not because reading and writing abilities improve as a consequence of repetition, but because the activities, if meaningfully undertaken, provides *opportunities* to learn. As cognitive psychologists are realizing more and more, it is what we know already that makes learning possible. The basis of learning is understanding. The best and most convenient support for reading is familiarity with the topic. Reading enhances familiarity with texts, an expansion of understanding that is the opposite of practicing a skill, of rote-memorizing some facts, or of stamping in a habit.

Indeed, the words *practice* and *exercise* can be appropriately used with respect to literacy, but not in the programmatic sense. Children should practice reading and writing in the way doctors practice medicine, or astronomers practice observing the sky, not as a drill but as an avocation. The possibilities of written language should be exercised, but only in the way in which we should exercise civil rights, by asserting what is our due.

The danger in using the word *skill* in conjunction with reading and writing is that it can justify teaching blindly through instruction and drill. Literacy is a matter not of honing skills but of increasing confidence, familiarity, and understanding, all consequences of meaningful use. A better metaphor for learning to read and to write than the acquisition of skills might be a growing acquaintance with a wide expanse of countryside or of a city neighborhood. And for such an acquaintance it is clear that experienced and collaborative guides are required, not drill, exercises, and tests.

## Levels and stages

Learning is often discussed as if it should move children from one place or altitude to another—"Johnny is still only reading at the third-grade level." Sometimes the same language is employed to explain why learning is not taking place—"Jane hasn't reached the concrete-operational stage yet." Children are classified as being at levels or stages, as if these were ladders to be clambered up one giant step at a time.

Consider all those children alleged to be at the prereading level or stage. There is an implication that they are inadequate or unformed in some way, that they require a particular course of treatment. But there is no prereading state that the brain can be in any more than there is a mental or physical state of pregeography or prealgebra. All the phrase can really mean is that the child is not familiar with reading, which is no more a perverse condition of the brain than an adult's ignorance of the domestic economy of Lithuania. In practice, the phrase is unlikely to mean anything more than that the child cannot make sense of a particular form of reading instruction. A child who does not know the names of the letters of the alphabet is still at the prereading stage if the instruction requires such knowledge. The fact that a child can be transformed from prereader to beginning reader overnight, through placement in a different classroom or with a different group, indicates that we are dealing with administrative matters, not mental states.

The most that reference to a prereading stage or level can really mean is that the child is not familiar with uses of written language. But such a reference would be highly imprecise and probably wrong. Familiarity with written language requires extensive insight into its functions and mechanisms, and recent research has demonstrated that even preschool children in many cultures have complex and subtle knowledge of these critical matters, without formal instruction. (For reviews of this research, see Goelman, Oberg and Smith, 1984). Such familiarity is acquired through experience, which means engaging in literate activities with more competent adults or peers, not through instruction, which is usually not available in any case. We were all prereaders once. Nothing we were formally taught enabled us to leap to the level or stage of being a reader. Understanding expands as literacy is made meaningful. The danger of talking about levels and stages is that what should be regarded as a smooth and natural progression is considered to be a series of halts or handicaps. The usual consequence of the "remediation" (another grossly inappropriate metaphor) that may be applied is greater deprivation of meaningful literacy experience.

The metaphor of level is widely overworked in the primary grades. Children are characterized as working at their own level, or below grade level, or reading at a third-grade level. Books are listed according to levels. But there are no levels at school, except possibly in the high jump. Many third-grade children can read books that some fourth graders cannot read, but cannot read some books that some second-grade children are able to read. These levels are at best averages or probabilities, computed—if they are actually computed at all—in the most abstract of ways on the most arbitrary of measures. They tell us nothing about whether a particular child will like or even understand a particular book. They ignore the fact that children and language are complex and individual.

Spelling is another popular habitat for stages. Children are categorized as being at the invented spelling stage and helped to get out of it (or discouraged from staying in it), as if invented spelling were an unavoidable but undesirable childish habit. But all adults who write invent spelling, when no other resource is available, and sometimes when it is. The general preference, I suppose, would be to spell every word correctly, though this should not be the most compelling concern during early drafts. But if we do not know a correct spelling—say for a name or word we have heard but never seen in print—then what do we do? Look it up in a dictionary or directory? Suppose we cannot find the word, or do not have the time to go in search of it? We do the best we can; we make a best guess. Are writers who do this regressing to a juvenile habit? Or are they making the most of limited resources? For children the situation is the same, whatever their age. When trying to write something they will employ correct spelling if they know it (and incorrect spelling if they make a mistake). But if they know they do not know a correct spelling, they will do the best they can. Occasionally it will be possible to look the word up, or to ask a teacher or friend. But often the best or only available strategy will be to make a guess, to invent a spelling—especially for creative and enthusiastic young writers. To say that such children have entered the invented-spelling stage, or reverted to it or got stuck in it, is again to mistake the nature of both children and writing.

Much of the tendency to locate children at stages can be

attributed to the genius and authority of Piaget. But Piaget intended that the term should be used descriptively, not in any fixed and explanatory manner. He was saying that children thought and behaved in particular ways that could be *called* stages, not *because* they were at a particular stage. In fact he was at pains to point out that the concept could not be used to predict behavior, but rather represented broad periods of development. Piaget was talking primarily about what children can only do in mature ways with prior knowledge, in the same way that their carpentry is clumsy until they are familiar with handling tools. The condition says nothing about the state or development of a child's brain.

There are no sudden changes in the structure or function of children's brains. What differs over time is the content of the brain, what the child knows. The appropriate remedy for a child who cannot do something is not drill to develop part of the brain, nor months of inactivity, but relevant experience. Experience that is meaningful expands familiarity and increases understanding, the basis of all learning.

A number of familiar terms accompany the concept of stages. One is the word *growth*, and another is the even more popular word *development*. Perhaps when such expressions are employed at their broadest extent—in talking of "personal growth," for example—their metaphorical function is most obvious and least dangerous. Minds do not grow like plants and trees, or even like our bodies. Minds do not need, or thrive on, the same kinds of nourishment and exercise that organs and limbs require. Minds expand as a consequence of experience, and the expansion is always specific to the experience. My intention here is not to endorse behavioristic stimulus-response theories of learning, which assert that environmental contingencies are responsible for everything we learn. Experience must always be comprehensible and relevant to each individual's purposes. It is not a fertilizer; it is learning itself.

The words *maturation* and *maturity* are often employed in the same way as *development* and *growth*, and they are equally meaningless and circular. It explains nothing to assert that children have not learned certain things because they are immature (though their immaturity may be explained by their not having learned certain things). Learning will not become easier if a child is left "to grow." Rather, learning takes care of maturity and growth. Obviously, anything we don't know now can only be learned when we are older. But the passage of time will not take care of the learning.

The only clue to whether a child is at a particular stage or level is what the child cannot do. And the only way to move out of that stage or level is through learning. Children, like everyone else, always know less about some things than some other people for the simple reason that they have not yet learned them, not because they have not grown enough. *Stages* and *levels* are perhaps the most disposable words and concepts in education, together with their ordering into *taxonomies* and *hierarchies*. They convey images of lurching from one unstable base to another. They suggest that sometimes children may not be capable of learning at all. The metaphor becomes the means and justification for pigeonholing children.

## Conclusion

What can be done about metaphors? I do not propose their abolition. We can no more do without metaphors in language than we could dispense with the glass in our windows and optical instruments. Metaphors enable us to perceive the world in meaningful ways. We could not say the things we want without them. But metaphors always distort; they can never be entirely appropriate or veridical. The distortion can be dangerous unless we are aware of it. The words I have been referring to are not ephemeral jargon (like *parameters, interface,* and *grass roots*). They are not buzzwords; they have become deeply embedded in our language use. And in any case, language cannot be legislated.

I have three suggestions. The first is always to be on the watch for metaphorical uses of language, to question them when they occur. Metaphors masquerade as explanations. Their authority evaporates when they are identified as analogies. It is usually much easier to look skeptically at an analogy than at a statement of fact. To say that the brain contains manufacturing machinery similar to that of industry would immediately provoke questions if not dissent. But casual assertions about processes in the brain can appear profound and impervious to criticism, which may be the reason for talking that way in the first place. Every metaphor carries ready-made meanings that slip past our guard unless scrutinized carefully.

My second suggestion is to seek and employ alternative metaphors, especially if their unfamiliarity will provoke a reaction. To inquire into the acquisition of reading skills is to approach a tired topic in a tired way, but to talk of the geography of reading or the harmonies of comprehension might at least raise curiosity about what exactly is being said. It is useful occasionally to question why particular metaphors arise in the first place. Metaphors for the brain and for society tend to reflect the conspicuous contemporary technology; today, obviously, computers. Why should this be, when so many alternatives are available? Why should learning be viewed as a matter of acquiring information, or as a process, when metaphors could be drawn from architecture or music?

The third suggestion is to convert metaphors into similes, to employ "like" or "as if" more frequently. To say that learning to read is *like* acquiring a skill—or even like any other skill—invites a deeper analysis. Talking about the process of writing is deceptively bland, but to say that writing is like a manufacturing process makes a strong assertion that can be challenged. Similes signal that statements should not be taken literally. They are like the stickers put on glass doors to warn people not to walk through them.

Metaphors conceal themselves. My three suggestions start from—indeed, depend upon—recognizing metaphors for what they are. Familiar metaphors are particularly difficult to detect. The contexts in which they lurk must be scrupulously examined if they are to be revealed. In other words—to avoid metaphors altogether for a moment—nothing about literacy, learning, and teaching should ever be taken for granted.

# How education backed the wrong horse

The vast discrepancy between the fluent way in which children naturally learn and the plodding and unproductive manner in which they are frequently treated in school is a topic I've already discussed several times in these essays. I have described how children learn continuously, and learn exactly what is demonstrated to them. Children learn collaboratively by apprenticing themselves to more experienced "members of the club" who help them to engage in activities that are manifestly worthwhile and meaningful. Children in school do not often see teachers engaged in meaningful reading or writing, or in any other activity that is not formal "instruction."

In place of club activities, schools offer instructional programs and tests. Prespecified objectives, not immediate relevance, determine what students and teachers must attend to next. Students are often taught and tested on one decontextualized thing at a time, in a predetermined sequence, in the false expectation that sooner or later this will make them expert readers and writers. Such mindless ritual has never been shown to produce anything but disabled learners, although it is the basis of the "excellence" that contemporary programmatic instruction is expected to "deliver."

The misguided development of programmatic instruction during the past thirty years can be directly traced to two factors, both coincidentally related to the early space program in the United States. The technological roots of programmatic instruction lie in systems analysis and program planning. The fractionation of major goals into sequences of small steps, which eventually took mankind to the moon and back, was expected to boost every American child into an orbit of literacy. The administrative foundations of programmatic instruction are those of taut centralized control, remote from the scene of operations, not unlike the "mission control" of space flights. Experts prescribe procedures and monitor performance to ensure that all components of the system meet specified objectives. In the name of "accountability," bureaucratic authorities at state (or provincial) and federal levels have continued to expand their control of education through the selection of curriculum and the imposition of tests and examinations to ensure compliance with the prescribed curriculum. I have discussed these pedagogical and political issues in detail in my book, *Insult to Intelligence* (1986).

While many individual teachers struggle against the encroachment of programmatic instruction and testing, for example through the "whole language" movement, education in general has been remarkably susceptible to the pressures of instructional programmers and to the blandishments of publishers in reading, writing, and other school subjects. Why has education succumbed so willingly to an alien technology, now so pervasive that many teachers and administrators cannot contemplate an alternative? What made education so vulnerable? The answer is that education considered its choices and made its decisions on the basis of an inappropriate theory. Every profession—every science and every art—needs a philosophy, a theoretical paradigm, on which to base its actions. Education made the wrong choice.

### The theoretical basis of education

For two thousand years until the beginning of the present century, the prevailing theory of Western education was classical. A thorough and disciplined immersion in literature and philosophy was expected to produce individuals who could think logically and know or find out everything they needed to know. Application to such a regime was assured by appeals to reason, bolstered not infrequently by corporal punishment. The approach was hardly scientific, and the spirit of the present century demanded that education follow a more "objective" route that would ensure learning. The technological age required not so much a philosophy of the *content* of education as a theory of the *process*. And it is here that education made the mistake from which it still may not recover. Education looked for a theory of learning—and it backed the wrong horse. It put its faith in experimental psychology. Psychology persuaded education that the way to teach was to break complex subjects down into small unrelated parts, to be practiced until tests showed that learning had occurred and to be reinforced by the immediate feedback of grades or other marks of approval.

Psychological learning theory has been the justification for so many educational decisions that once again many people cannot imagine that there could be any other reasonable choice. Education is concerned with learning, and learning is a large part, if not the central focus, of psychology. How could this be misleading? So I want to show why psychology is the wrong horse—why psychology has totally misled itself as well as others on this crucial matter of learning. I shall also show that there are other runners in the field to which education might have turned, and even could now be trying to turn at this late stage, before psychology's theory of learning encourages computer-controlled instruction that could destroy education completely.

PSYCHOLOGY AND LEARNING

Psychology has never been comfortable with learning. When psychology developed out of philosophy and physiology as an independent academic discipline barely a hundred years ago, learning was taken for granted. There is no historical *tradition* of studying learning as a process. Philosophers might worry and argue minutely about the relationships of sensation and perception, about the world in the head and the world outside, even about what individuals should learn, but no one ever asked what learning *was*, or how it could be ensured. Physiologists similarly looked for functions in the brain underlying the maintenance of bodily systems and the expression of emotions, but that the brain learned was never questioned. Areas of the brain were mapped to account for many sensory, perceptual, motor, and cognitive activities, but a specialized learning function was not even considered. What was the brain, if it was not a learning organ? When phrenologists, who could project any kind of mental ability they liked onto the bumpy surfaces of the skull, claimed to identify prominences associated with thirty or more affective and intellectual faculties, learning was not one of them.

Yet when psychology was born, learning quickly became one of its central concerns. The first words of the second edition of Ernest Hilgard's classic *Theories of Learning* (1956), assert that "the scientific study of learning is carried on primarily by psychologists. . . . Professional educators have welcomed educational psychology as a foundation science upon which to build their practices, and studies of learning have gone on concurrently in laboratories of general psychology and laboratories of educational psychology, with interplay between the pure and applied fields. Under the circumstances, it is very natural for psychologists to feel that the study of learning belongs to them."

The emphasis on the word "laboratories" in Hilgard's description is significant. Psychologists at the end of the nineteenth century sought to establish their discipline as a *science* by emulating the experimental and computational procedures of their colleagues in the laboratories of the physical sciences. Counting and measurement were regarded as the epitome of scientific behavior, and even today many psychologists do not believe that theorizing about behavior is valid unless it can be subjected to experimental tests (or simulated on a computer), with every variable under control. Simple observation and induction are anathema to them.

The problem confronting early psychologists was to find aspects of behavior amenable to being counted or measured in a "scientific" way. The passage I have just quoted from Hilgard continues, "A scientist, along with the desire to satisfy his curiosity about the facts of nature, has a predeliction for ordering his facts into systems of laws and theories. He is interested not only in verified facts and relationships, but in neat and parsimonious ways of summarizing these facts." In other words, only certain kinds of facts, organized in particular ways, attract the experimentalist's attention; everything else is ignored. Experimental psychologists *impose* their procrustean framework on what they study.

Early psychologists discovered two fruitful areas for experimental study, both rather surprisingly. One was the classical philosophical question of the relation between sensation and perception, which proved to be remarkably tractable to examination through the measurement of "reaction-times." Psychologists could compare, for example, how many milliseconds it took an experimental subject to decide that *something* had been seen or heard (sensation) compared with deciding *what* had been seen or heard (perception). Until the computer arrived to take care of the timing and scoring, no one could be called an experimental psychologist who did not carry a stopwatch.

The other area that proved fertile to experimental psychologists, perhaps even more remarkably, was learning. Untouched by philosophy and physiology, and indeed by any other science, learning lay waiting to be exploited—if only it could be brought under experimental control. But how could researchers measure how long it takes to learn something? How fast people learn depends on their individual interests and past experience. And what is a "unit" of learning? How could an experimenter compare how long it takes one person to learn to speak French with how long it takes another to learn to ride a bicycle, or even to compare learning the past participle of one irregular French verb with learning that there is one particular component of a bicycle called a sprocket?

The problem was solved in the late 1870s by a German, Hermann Ebbinghaus, who is generally acknowledged to be the father of experimental psychology, the person who made it possible for psychology to become a science (Hilgard, 1956; Boring, 1957). Ebbinghaus's solution was a masterstroke. If what makes learning difficult to bring into the experimental laboratory is individual interest and relevance, then all interest and relevance should be removed from what is to be learned. If experimental subjects are given *meaningless* materials to learn—like the syllables TAV, ROP, or ZEG—then everyone begins from the same place and has the same amount of learning to accomplish. According to historian of psychology Edwin Boring (1957), no one had thought of anything even remotely like the nonsense syllable before Ebbinghaus—a fact that in itself might be regarded as significant.

Suddenly, experiments in learning became replicable. One group of subjects required to learn a list of nonsense syllables (or nonsense shapes or nonsense sounds) performed no differently from other groups given a similar task. Psychology had its first scientific laws—the now venerable Laws of Learning. Learning and forgetting became predictable phenomena. Learning was a simple function of the number of items to be learned and the number of practice trials. Forgetting depended on how much time had passed since the last learning trial. But it was all based on nonsense. Sense turns experimental results upside down. The only predictable thing about meaningful materials is that learning takes place sooner and forgetting is much slower. Normal, sensible learning is excluded from the research laboratory.

It should not be surprising that psychology's Laws of Learning were so appealing to the proponents of a "scientific" approach to education. Psychology had shown that learning could be guaranteed—for a short while at least—if fragments of what was to be learned were presented and practiced one at a time. Meaningful learning could not be organized in such a controlled and replicable manner—and the instructional programmer was no more entranced by uncontrolled learning than the experimental psychologist. Learning became a matter of "trials to criterion." If a student does not learn the first time, the task should be repeated until learning occurs, no matter how bored or confused the task makes the learner.

All of this is based on theories derived from unnatural and difficult learning, controlled by an outsider and stripped of sense, relevance, and utility, in which there is little possibility of personal involvement. Individuals do not normally learn in artificially contrived and manipulated situations but in communal activities. Instead of facilitating learning, the technology and testing of programmatic instruction does everything possible to hinder it.

Benjamin Bloom (1976) introduced to education the notion that learning is simply a matter of "time on task"—a rule that applies only to nonsense. If someone does not learn something quickly and effortlessly it is probably because what is being taught does not make sense. But instead of supplying more sense, instructional programmers demanded more time, and offered more nonsense. Students who couldn't learn lists of nonsense were "diagnosed" as suffering from "learning disabilities"—located, like the old phrenological faculties, in specific areas of the brain.

Bloom (1956) had earlier proposed his influential "taxonomy of learning," which is the basis of so much contemporary teaching and testing. According to Bloom's taxonomy, "stimulus-response" learning—the rote memorization of facts—is the easiest kind of learning, and applying and evaluating knowledge the most difficult. But the taxonomy is based on nonsense-learning, and is again upside down. In the world outside the experimental laboratory or programmatic classroom, rote learning of nonsensical material is the most difficult and inefficient, while those things that we find worthwhile and useful are the easiest to learn.

REINFORCEMENT AND NONSENSE

Bloom himself acknowledges B. F. Skinner, the best-known contemporary proponent of *behaviorism*, as the primary source of his educational insights. Behaviorism is the other flank of experimental psychology's study of learning—a "science of behavior" that relates learning to the external control of events, to "contingencies of reinforcement." The insights of behaviorism are based entirely on rats, pigeons, and other animals. And not on animals in natural surroundings, but in cages, in the "Skinner boxes" that were the world's first teaching machines. Even animals must be constrained to learn nonsense if they are to contribute to psychology as a science.

Behaviorism's animal studies were responsible for the other great law that psychology donated to education, the Law of Effect. This law states that learning will not take place in the absence of motivation, and that incentives and rewards are essential if learning is to take place. The law ignores the fact that most human learning takes place in the absence of extrinsic motivation or reward, and that motivation does not guarantee learning. We are unaware of most of the things we learn, and many of the things people have the most difficulty learning are those they are most motivated to learn. Motivation and reinforcement are only required for nonsense-learning or for other kinds of pointless or painful activity—which is the reason Skinner maintained his experimental animals at 80 percent of their normal body weight and rewarded their learning with pellets of food.

Learning and motivation are not the only aspects of behavior that experimental psychology has distorted, to the detriment of those in education who believe that psychology says everything that needs to be said about learning. As cognitive psychologist George Mandler (1985) has recently pointed out, emotion is another aspect of human behavior that has been completely left out of consideration in the experimental laboratory. Emotion is an intrinsic part of learning, but it can also be unpredictable and is therefore not permitted to confound learning experiments. Until recently, studies of emotional behavior were relegated to "abnormal psychology." And "special education" is the area in which emotional behavior in the classroom is generally placed. Anyone who becomes emotional over learning or failure to learn has a "behavioral problem."

Most "problem-solving" studies are also based on unnatural laboratory situations. Experimental subjects, both human and animal, are confronted with tasks they would not normally encounter and which are often deliberately misleading, requiring judgments the subjects are not usually called upon to make.

## THE UNNATURAL STUDY OF MEMORY

Psychologists have also persuaded both themselves and educators that *remembering* is difficult and effortful. This again is a distorted and misleading point of view. Most of the time we remember what we need to know accurately, automatically, and effortlessly. We do not usually have difficulty remembering our own name, or where we live, or our telephone number. We remember our own birthday and that of a few other people as well; we remember holidays. We remember our friends' names, and how they look, and where they live, and some of their telephone numbers. We remember everything about the world that is familiar to us. We remember that trees are called *trees* and birds *birds*, even if we can't remember the names of specific kinds. We remember the meanings of every word we know, how these words are pronounced, and how many of them are spelled as well. We remember innumerable things.

Memory is not a special faculty of the brain that functions only occasionally, and often not particularly efficiently. All of our everyday life depends on memory, but this continuous kind of remembering is so effortless and usually so efficient that even psychologists have been tempted to give it a different name. They want to differentiate it from the kind of memory tested in the experimental laboratory—and in school examinations.

Mandler (1985) wants to call everyday remembering "reminding"—though he does not want to say that it is different from any other kind of memory. In fact, Mandler suggests that apparent differences of memory are really only differences in forms of test. If we examine something shortly after it has come to our attention we talk about "short-term memory." If we examine something over a longer period we refer to "long-term memory." If the question concerns factual knowledge, some psychologists would refer to "semantic memory," while a test related to specific events would be denoted as "episodic memory." But it is all the same memory, Mandler proposes. And that memory is not a special mental faculty that is different from learning or perception or "thinking." Memory is a part of all learning, perception, and thinking, inevitably and usually unconsciously.

Just as with learning, the conditions that invoke fluent memorization are meaningfulness, utility, and personal involvement. We learn most easily when something is relevant, when it is useful, makes sense, and we have no fear of failing to learn. And we remember most easily when what we need to recall is most relevant and useful, and we have no anxiety about not remembering. Some theorists—myself included—characterize *thinking* in this way. They assert that *prediction* is the basis of all behavior, that we construct possible realities before we enter them. Our memories arise on cue before we need to act and guide our actions.

Of course, memory lets us down sometimes. We fail to remind ourselves to buy something at the store on the way home, or to make a telephone call that we had planned. Often there is an explanation of why we forget—we are distracted, or confused, or possibly even may not want to remember, and we somehow suppress the recall. If we fail to recall something it is usually not because we have suffered a permanent loss of memory. We just can't get access to it for the moment (like the word that stays on the wrong side of the tip of our tongue but that we recognize the moment somebody mentions it). And sometimes memory is frustratingly difficult. Remembering becomes difficult when it is conscious, when we *deliberately* try to remember something that has not sprung to mind at once.

"Easy" and "difficult" remembering differ in the way they are invoked. Easy remembering occurs involuntarily, in the normal everyday course of events. Difficult remembering is the kind we engage in deliberately, because we "want" to remember something that we haven't conveniently reminded our-selves of, or because someone else wants us to remember something that is not part of our ongoing frame of reference. Memory becomes difficult when we try to take charge of it.

When we deliberately try to remember something we are in a sense approaching it from the wrong end. Instead of allowing the memory to rise from the way the brain is currently making sense of the world, we try to dig down to it from the outside. Deliberate remembering is usually too contrived to be effective. And the most deliberate and contrived efforts to manipulate memory occur when the control is in the hands of someone else—when we are told to bring something to mind. The worst conditions for memory, like the worst conditions for learning, are when someone else tells us precisely what we should be doing.

And now comes the irony. It is precisely this difficult, delib-erate, relatively uncommon aspect of memory that experimen-tal psychology has studied. In fact, much of psychology's concern with memory has been with the *failure* to remember, and with forgetting. The consequence has been that many people, es-pecially those who have studied psychology, have been led to believe that remembering—like learning—is difficult and typ-ically unsuccessful. Psychology's study of memory has been like its study of learning—an obsessive focus on the difficult and deliberate rather than on the fluent and unconscious. And the vision has been restricted for the same reason—for exper-imental control. The experimenter in a memory experiment usually tells subjects what they should recall. Anything they remember that has nothing to do with the experiment is an intrusion. Subjects are probably remembering all the time they are engaged in the experiment—they remember that the sun is shining outside the laboratory, that they have a luncheon appointment, and other interesting things they might otherwise be doing—but they are only rated as "remembering" if they recall the "items" nominated by the experimenter.

## LEARNING AS A SOCIAL ACTIVITY

Learning and remembering are usually associated with the in-dividual. We don't expect other people to learn for us, and we usually expect our own brains to remind us of what we want to know. But such an egocentric view is misleading. We are not responsible for most of our own learning or for jogging our own memory, except for the fact that we might put ourselves in situations where the learning and remembering are invoked. We learn when we are engaged in activities with other people—even if the other people involved might be as physically remote as an author or artist. Situations in which we are engaged invoke the memories that come to mind for us. Learning and remembering are both social events.

The obsession with experimental control in psychological and educational research has resulted in a focus on isolated individuals, like the rat in the Skinner box. Experimentalists have had very little concern for how people learn in groups, and especially for how they learn from and with the aid of others. (In the experimental laboratory, as in the formal classroom, mutual assistance is usually regarded as "cheating.") Psychology puts only *individuals* into the learning laboratory. Even if a number of subjects are engaged in a study at the same time, they are usually separated and warned not to collaborate with each other. Education does the same thing—everyone at his or her own desk, with a personal notebook, personal worksheets, and of course, a personal record of scores and grades. (Educational procedures and language have a remarkable resemblance to those of experimental laboratories.) Misconceived "individualization" is even easier now that students can work at their own computer workstations, shielded from each other.

Both education and experimental psychology have overlooked the social nature of learning. We learn through apprenticeships, through collaboration, when someone else shows us that something is worth doing and helps us to do it ourselves. To study and facilitate learning we should not attempt to control it; rather we should do everything possible to encourage learning to flourish.

Piaget knew this. Piaget studied children's learning literally at their level, as he knelt among them to enter their world. He didn't try to force children to learn what he thought they ought to know, but he explored what they learned in normal situations and how these situations contributed to what they learned. His conclusion was that children learned, in their own way, all the time—by a process of interaction with the environment so natural he called it *adaptation*. Piaget has never been popular with experimental psychologists; he was not sufficiently "scientific" for them. And when experimental psychologists tried to replicate Piaget's findings in laboratory experiments, not surprisingly they often got different results. And education, unfortunately, when it has paid attention to Piaget at all, has tended to do so narrowly, looking at the "levels" or "stages" that children of various ages should or should not be able to attain rather than at the conditions that facilitate learning.

Piaget was not the only psychologist who observed children without disturbing their natural behavior. This unobtrusive methodology was the technique of the "developmental psycholinguists" who first explored the astounding amounts children learn about their first language, some of which I have described in the opening essay. These researchers studied infant language development by the painstaking method of recording and analyzing everything that children said, rather than by assessing their performance on tests of materials that the children had been given to learn.

Like Piaget, developmental psychologists recognize that experimental manipulation distorts data. Instead of observing how subjects react to what researchers want them to learn, they observe how the individuals interact with the world around them. Some researchers even pay attention to what other people around the learner are doing. To many experimental psychologists, such researchers are insufficiently rigorous; they are not scientific. But in fact, they are employing techniques adopted from a different science. They are employing the methodology of anthropology.

Anthropology is the other horse that education could have backed. Instead of putting its faith in the limited manipulations of experimental psychology, education could have paid more attention to the broader, less obtrusive insights of the discipline that studies relations among *people*.

### The alternative

Unlike experimental psychologists, cultural anthropologists have long recognized that it is impossible to study a situation objectively if investigators intrude their own rules, desires, or frames of reference.

The principal research method anthropologists have developed is *ethnography*, meaning the description of cultures. Ethnography is the term that is beginning to be heard in education as the most appropriate way to study learning. Other terms used for similar or related approaches include "qualitative analysis" (as opposed to quantitative analysis), "thick description," "participant observation," "open-ended interviewing," "in-depth interviewing," "phenomenological research," and "the case study method" (see Bogdan and Biklen, 1982). I would characterize the approach as *trying to see the world from the other person's point of view*. In an educational context, Yetta Goodman calls it simply "kid-watching."

Margaret Mead (1976), for example, took learning for granted in her anthropological studies of cultures in the South Pacific and in American schools. She had observed quite simply that children learned what they saw other people do, from the community activities they were initiated into, *if the children themselves wanted and expected to be able to do those things*. Mead didn't inquire into the imagined mental processes by which the children learned, but she observed the circumstances, the *culture* of the learning situation. She didn't ask *how* children managed to remember what they were taught but *what* they remembered. She looked at the apprenticeships, the collaborations, the interpersonal relations, the attitudes. Her conclusion, very briefly, was that children learned and remembered when they were involved in adult activities they saw as attainable and worthwhile. Learning had nothing to do with how many drills or exercises the children were given or with how often they were tested. If children were not interested in learning, or were discouraged, adults tried to stimulate their involvement and self-confidence rather than treating them as defective.

Anthropologists are becoming active in contemporary studies of literacy, in and out of school. Among the most prominent are Shirley Brice Heath, author of *Ways with Words* (1983), and Hope Jensen Leichter, editor of *The Family as Educator* (1974), both of whom have chapters in *Awakening to Literacy* (Goelman, Oberg and Smith, 1984). Kid-watching has resulted in some milestone publications in literacy study in recent years, such as Glenda Bissex's *Gnys at Wrk* (1980), Denny Taylor's *Family Literacy* (1983), and Lucy Calkins's aptly named *Lessons from a Child* (1983). Watching how children learn to talk, to read, and to write in nonmanipulative conditions has led to the development of the "psycholinguistic" and "whole language" philosophies, which are currently struggling against the centralized standardized technologies of teaching and testing that threaten to swamp our classrooms.

The participant-observer approach of reading and writing *with* children offers a way of learning many teachers employ intuitively but which can be formalized. More and more ethnographic theses are being completed in education and psychology, although it is not always easy to make such research acceptable in the faculties where "scientific" and "controlled" are still synonymous terms.

The approach also gives teachers a way to find out about themselves and about students, as exemplified in the work in Britain of Joan Tough (1976). Other leading United Kingdom researchers who have made contributions influential on both sides of the Atlantic with nonintrusive studies of students, teachers, and school practices include Douglas Barnes, James Britton, Connie and Harold Rosen, and Margaret Spencer.

Because educational planners and instructional designers have been more influenced by the psychological model of learning than by the anthropological, schools are often concerned with all the wrong things. Teachers and administrators worry about performance, not attitude or proclivity. As Shirley Brice Heath (1985) says, "We have given only nodding acknowledgement to the touchy question of 'what is the context for learning literate behaviors, as distinguished from learning literacy skills?' " If we want children to read and write, ethnography tells us we should be concerned with making reading and writing interesting to them. Then they'll learn the relevant skills better than we could ever deliberately teach them. When students are *forced* to learn to read and write, then reading and writing become aversive to them. It's the same with science, or anything else we try to teach. Every teacher knows it's easy to teach a child who is interested, yet the technology of education, experimental psychology's legacy, says that interest is irrelevant; it is the student's responsibility, not the primary concern of the teacher.

All educators must recognize that the theories of learning underlying the mechanical programs and repetitive tests of contemporary education are misleading, unnatural, and dangerous. Learning is a social activity, and its most important aspects from the learner's point of view are the other people in the situation, the "club" that the learner must join. Teachers can best learn all of this by looking at students—and by looking at themselves and other teachers—from an anthropological perspective. They must ask "What is going on here?" not in terms of a lesson plan or curriculum objectives but in terms of a student trying to make sense of the world. Then teachers must persuade each other and the administrators who control so much of what they do in classrooms that ethnography rather than experimental psychology is the right horse for education to back.

# Postscripts

**Can anything be done for children who don't want to join the literacy club?**

Children who don't want to join the club are the only ones we need do anything for. Those who are in the club—who see themselves as readers and writers, and who read—will become literate without any further direct help. Therefore a teacher's basic role in literacy education might be seen as encouraging children who don't want to, or who feel there is no place for them, to join the club.

Reluctant readers and writers—like "disabled" readers and writers—can't be forced. No one can be coerced into literacy, or into showing an interest in reading and writing. And irrelevant rewards—"extrinsic reinforcement"—will fail as well. Show a child that the payoff for reading or writing something is a treat, a token, a happy face, or a high mark, and that is what the child will learn is the price literacy should extract. Every child knows that anything accompanied by coercion, no matter how benign, cannot be worth doing in its own right.

There are two requirements for bringing reluctant children into the literacy club—and they are the same as the requirements for attracting anyone into any club. The first is to make the club interesting, which is basically achieved when teachers demonstrate that they know something the children don't know, attracting their curiosity and arousing their desire. Of course, teachers won't do this if they never feel free to read a book silently in class, just for themselves, so they can say to their students, "Look, just keep quiet for the next five minutes. I want to finish this chapter." How often do children hear teachers say, "Could you help me finish this *poem* (or short story, or film script, or opera) I've been working on?" Teachers must make their own values explicit. Children are always intrigued by things that adults *enjoy* doing—how else would they acquire all the habits we would rather they did not learn?

The second requirement is to make the club accessible, to show that every child can join. One of the paradoxes of contemporary education is that children able to participate in formal school activities fairly effortlessly get lots of opportunity and encouragement while those who have problems or negative attitudes get fewer interesting experiences, relatively more difficult assignments, and more failure and discouragement. Obviously, many of the constraints on reluctant readers and writers come from the structured and competitive nature of contemporary schooling. "Low marks" automatically exclude children from the literacy club—in the eyes of their teachers, parents, classmates, and in their own eyes too. Not only will such children find it more difficult to obtain meaningful demonstrations and collaboration, but they will rationalize that they don't want these things in any case, that reading and writing are "boring," and that their exclusion from the club is their own decision.

To open the club to such students, teachers must take particular pains to make its activities distinctive from routine classroom activities, from the deadening aura of "school work"—no coercion, no scores or grades, and sympathetic collaboration from teachers and other students, not in *teaching* reading and writing, but in *doing* interesting things with reading and writing. (The best collaborators for reluctant or "disabled" readers are frequently older students—or people from outside the school—who themselves experienced difficulty with literacy. They are more likely to behave like helpers, less like invigilators, and in the process, they learn more about reading and writing themselves.)

Reading and writing can be introduced to children in a variety of ways—there are innumerable entrances to the literacy club. The trick is to find something involving reading and writing that interests the learner and to engage the learner authentically in that area of interest, making the reading and writing incidental. Lack of interest in reading and writing should not be a problem, because it should never be an issue.

Reading can be such an interesting activity for everyone in some respects, and writing can be so satisfying personally, that children should find entry into the literacy club as natural and effortless as entry into the club of talkers. Nevertheless with some children there will be difficulties. They may already have associated reading and writing with boredom and failure. Parents or other teachers may have impressed upon them the more tedious aspects of literacy instruction, making obstacle courses rather than clubs out of reading and writing. And indiscriminate television watching can function like a drug, leaving its addicts listless and uninterested. No one can guarantee swift success. Sometimes when patterns of mutual frustration and discouragement have become too deeply engrained, a solution can only begin with a change of teacher.

Getting into the literacy club is no different for reluctant children than for the enthusiastic ones. It just requires more patience and sensitivity.

### How long is it necessary for teachers to read to children?

Some teachers seem to fear that reading to students, or writing for them, will make students dependent. These teachers are afraid the students will always expect other people to do their reading and writing for them. But no learner has that much patience or passivity. The moment children feel they can read or write well enough to do what they want to do for themselves—often long before adults might think they are ready to do so—then they reject the helping hand. It is no different when children learn to ride a bicycle. Children never want to be pushed when they think they can pedal away for themselves (except when the going is uphill).

Teachers need not read to learners at all—if they can find someone else to do so. But someone must do the learners' reading for them until they are able to read a few things for themselves, and they are ready to learn to read by reading. Reading to children need not take long—only until they can read enough for authors to take over. Very little actual reading ability is required for this to occur, if the right kinds of interesting and familiar materials are available (for details of such materials, ask a child). Indeed, for a child to know the stories in advance by heart may be enough to turn the child over to the authors. What matters is the learner's *engagement*—reading known or familiar texts like an experienced reader.

I have not seen any formal research on the subject, but the

consensus I have detected, based on Paulo Freire's (1972) experiences with illiterate adults in the Amazonian jungle and on the work of Margaret Spencer (1987), plus interviews with many successful teachers, is that students can read independently in—*six weeks*. Six weeks' assisted reading is all that is required before authors can take over. Unfortunately, some students can spend twelve years in school and never experience those six weeks.

A few teachers have disputed my estimate. They have told me that six weeks is too long, that it takes four weeks or less for a child to become an independent reader. Some have insisted that children go home on Friday afternoon unable to read and come back on Monday morning reading. There is no doubt that children can make incredible progress once their attention is seized by reading and they feel confident enough to read by themselves. Indeed, I am now prepared to contemplate what I once dismissed as unlikely, that some children actually teach themselves to read without any outside assistance at all. They are able to put themselves into the hands of helpful authors from the beginning, because of their prior knowledge of the story or rhyme, or the clues provided by illustrations.

Jane Torrey (1969) has described how the writers of labels and television commercials might help children to learn to read by themselves. Spontaneous self-admission into the literacy club may even explain how children succeed in learning to read when subjected to intensive classroom regimes of phonics and basal reader activities (which then of course get the credit for the achievement).

### Aren't you simply promoting whole language?

"Whole language" has become a label, and I try to avoid being labeled. When people argue in terms of labels and slogans, thought is inhibited rather than expanded. Once you are identified as a "whole language" person—or any other label—you are categorized and no one need any longer wonder what exactly you are talking about.

I am naturally sympathetic to whole-language teachers. I have worked with many of them, learned from them, and I have probably contributed to their philosophy myself—or at least supported their endeavors—by many of the things I have said and written in the past. But that is what whole language is—a philosophy, not a slogan or a method of teaching reading. Yet whole language has become so successful, or at least so conspicuous, that to many people it has become a method, something to be done, not something to be thought about.

Whole language began as a resistance movement among teachers who rejected the notion that artificial and fragmented bits of language could provide appropriate experience from which children would learn to read and write. These teachers also rejected the dismantling of language arts into specific skills and the constant testing that accompanies such instruction.

The philosophy has spread like a summer brushfire, with the sparks of its label "whole language" igniting dry tinder ahead of the core of the blaze. Regional conferences of thousands of whole-language teachers are not unusual. But with the expansion of whole-language awareness has come dilution and even distortion. Some teachers will say they are "doing whole language" if they use "big books" or "integrate" reading and writing activities. They still employ worksheets and engage in other artificial, trivialized activities. Publishers have begun to produce whole-language materials—a contradiction in terms—and the travesty of whole-language tests has begun to appear.

A host of new buzzwords has become prominent in prescribed frameworks and curriculum guides—words like *integrated, comprehensive, interactive, student-centered, balanced, coordinated*—all of which are supposed to reflect a "whole-language approach." Such words can justify any reactionary activity. They are language to avoid thinking.

I cannot support labels or slogans. Teachers must understand what they are doing. Teachers make the difference, not prescriptions, materials, or activities. It is better that a teacher be ignorant of the labels but understand that children learn by being engaged in meaningful and worthwhile activities than glib with the jargon but totally insensitive to the underlying realities.

### Give an example of what you consider creative possibilities for computers in schools.

I recently joined a group of teachers in Ontario, Canada, learning about a computer "networking" program devised by former school superintendent Patrick O'Kelly. The program, which runs on ordinary desk-top computers, offers remarkable new possibilities for research as well as for learning to use language, and it could be the basis of a new way of talking with people. In the demonstration there were six computers in a classroom, operated by small groups of people or by individuals. The computers could be in different rooms in the same school, or in different schools, or in factories, studios, or offices. But in some ways, the most interesting and perhaps the most useful possibilities arise when the computers and the participants are in the same room.

The screen on the monitor of each computer is divided into six rectangular "windows," one for each of the six operators or groups of operators, identified by the code names the operators devise for themselves. Everything written on the keyboard of each computer appears, letter by letter as it is typed, in the appropriate window on every screen, provided all the parties involved agree. Initially (and it is only initially) something may have to be done to get everyone communicating. In the demonstration, Patrick O'Kelly suggested that we try to find a couple of coincidences between any of our groups.

I need not detail the kinds of things that people started writing or the ways in which the exchanges became lively and even intimate as we all chatted away on our keyboards and watched the screen to read what everyone else was writing. The important thing is that everyone started writing—chatting on the screen—with interest and without inhibition. "Conversations" began. Some groups began exchanging messages between themselves, ignoring everything else. Some started asking for particular responses from all of the groups or from individuals. And at any time, a printer could produce a record of everything that had been said, not computer by computer, but statement by statement, with each "speaker" identified, so that we finished up with a script, a record of all the exchanges. We could see who initiated particular discussions and the kinds of responses that were provoked.

None of this is difficult. It is surprisingly easy to keep an eye on the five other windows, or to focus attention on the one that interests you. If you miss something of interest, you can "scroll" back the contents of a window as far and as often as you like.

Consider all this from a linguistic point of view. It is a *new* way of communicating. Six people, or groups of people, can talk simultaneously, without interfering with what anyone else is saying or attending to. Individuals need no longer be excluded from a discussion because someone with a more insistent manner is hogging the floor. Everyone gets an equal opportunity to participate, and the most interesting and relevant ideas, not the loudest voice, attract the most attention. Oddly enough, sharing ideas in this way can be easier and more effective than having six people sitting round a table trying to talk face to face. Those who *do* want to talk face to face can always leave their computers or look over the tops of them.

There are other interesting linguistic consequences. Language changes. Spelling and punctuation tend to be ignored, or become simplified, but not to the extent that other people can't read what is written. A new grammar emerges, not necessarily less complex than that of conventional spoken or written language, but more appropriate to the medium. And because there can be no "tone of voice" to express emphasis, graphic possibilities are devised and recruited—centering, capitalizing or italicizing, using stars, exclamation marks, and less conventional symbols. There is *learning*—individuals adopt the styles and signals of the people around them, providing a microscopic glimpse of the universal process of the cultural development of linguistic conventions.

Consider it from a learning point of view. People may talk more openly across the computer lines than they would if they were talking face to face to you. On the other hand, you can have access to what other people are thinking without letting them distract you. You can observe a short story being written, a song being composed. You might even be allowed to participate, to make suggestions and see them incorporated. Imagine writing a poem on such a system. If you wish, friendly observers may make suggestions that could help you, at the time they might help most, which you can easily adopt if you wish to but which you can also ignore without difficulty. These are new possibilities in writing or in any form of creative endeavor.

If you don't want everyone to see what you are writing, the touch of a function key will pull a "blind" down over your window on the screens of the other computers, and you have the privacy to do what you like. You can prevent your contributions from being included in any subsequent printout. You can get a printout of your own remarks that ignores what everyone else has said. If you want a private conversation with the operators of one of the other computers, you can easily shut everyone else out. No one can interfere with what you are doing, or what you have done, unless you permit them to. I don't know if it is currently possible—I've just thought of it—but provision could be made for people to make anonymous contributions—a communal window where unidentified comments could be expressed. Any other objections or useful suggestions that the devisers of the program have not anticipated can probably be accommodated on the spot, by the users themselves, without too much difficulty.

All this is *power*, not over other people but at your own fingertips, to facilitate or accomplish some of the things you personally want to achieve, to express or discuss, in interesting and collaborative ways. In classrooms where the program I have described has been installed, students check for messages and start talking to each other over the network as soon as they arrive every morning—reading and writing—even though they may have walked in talking side by side. Special education students wrote more on their own initiative than they did in regular class time. A teacher said that if the program were to be taken out of his school, he'd have a riot on his hands.

I have described one use of computers, which I experienced almost by chance. Many other systems of equal potential are available or being developed, not just in language and communication, but in art and design, music and drama, science and engineering. But whether they are used productively depends on the way that teachers who might use them understand learning and computers. The systems are not—and should not be—teacher proof.

I had expected crowds at the demonstration in which I participated because it was given at a conference attended by six hundred teachers. But only a dozen came. When I suggested to another group at the same conference who did not attend the demonstration that they must be either very sophisticated about computers, or very apprehensive, they nodded their heads for the latter. Many more teachers must become members of the computer club, so that they can be in charge of how computers are used in their classrooms.

## What do you regard as the greatest danger in education today?

In one word—*evaluation*. No matter how "liberated" teachers and administrators may become in their choice of materials and activities for classrooms, in the enlightened manner in which they "integrate the language arts," and in the support given to children who encounter problems in learning, students continue to be denied admission to the literacy club through the blight of constant monitoring and testing. Unfortunately, testing and grading are widely regarded as *good things*. Even people who recognize that evaluation can be harmful still frequently think that it is necessary. So instead of trying to reduce evaluation they seek "better" ways of doing it, and they do more of it. They feel there must be evaluation for the learner's benefit. But even when conducted "informally," evaluation inevitably has negative consequences and is never necessary.

Students behave differently in the face of evaluation. Teachers behave differently. And so do parents and principals. There is tension before major tests, palpable in every classroom and sometimes lasting for weeks, anxiety during the test, apprehension until the results are out, and deflation afterwards. It is the same on a smaller but cumulative basis for classroom tests and marks for assignments. Even *positive* evaluation depresses performance in educational contexts. Students who are used to getting high grades for their performances are discouraged and resentful when they get a low one and are reluctant to act if they get no evaluation at all. An evaluation is like a rubber stamp reading, "This is a ritualized school activity."

It is argued that there is constant evaluation in the world outside school. That is true—but it is a different kind of evaluation, done for different purposes, and with different consequences. Evaluation outside school is related strictly to fitness for purpose, to appropriateness for the occasion, not to assessing relative standards of achievement or comparative ability. (Where there is evaluation to measure achievement or make comparative judgments, it is generally undergone voluntarily, as in various sporting, artistic, or commercial contests, or to meet certain professional requirements or college admission. Individuals are not normally evaluated in discriminatory ways against their will—outside school.)

Evaluation out of school does not compare one person with another, but rather determines whether a particular behavior or product reaches a conventional standard. Are my clothes suitable for the occasion, will the shelf I have built bear the weight that is put upon it, is the article I have just written acceptable for publication? And the consequence of failing to meet conventional or expected standards is not the implicit reprimand of a score on a record but *help* to do the inadequate thing properly.

Even in the world of work, we are likely to receive collaboration almost every time we attempt to do something and fail—until it is decided that we really don't belong to the club (a dismaying situation indeed). Fortunately, children are rarely ejected from a club outside of school because they are not good enough. It is taken for granted that they will be unlikely to do anything that meets conventional adult standards, and they are likely to be given more assistance than they sometimes want or need to do better. People insist on helping them to make the model, finish the drawing, or put on their clothes. Children themselves do not expect to do things at adult levels of competence; they know they have not been around long enough. And they also know that for something important they can usually depend on adult or peer collaboration; they are natural apprentices.

It is only in school that the consequences of negative evaluation is invariably exclusion from the club, discouragement, and discrimination, and that the emphasis is on engaging in precisely those activities that one cannot do very well, in the most boring and unproductive ways. Even "informal" evaluation has inevitable consequences of disapprobation. Children have to be told about every spelling and punctuation mistake they make, even though their endeavor might have been to construct a thrilling story or a moving poem. They can become so concerned about their spelling and punctuation that they never again try to write another story or poem. It is a myth that a child who "gets away with a mistake" will not learn to correct that mistake in the future. As I explained in the first two essays in this collection, children constantly learn without correction through the collaboration of other members of the club to which they are admitted.

The essence of the problem of evaluation is the view that *anything a child can't do now must be taught*. If we could get away from that perception, then evaluation would be harmless. But in that case, evaluation as it is carried out in schools would also be unnecessary. Earlier in this book I referred to the assertion of Vygotsky (1978)—based on rigorous research studies—that anything children can do with help today they will be able to do unaided tomorrow, provided of course that they are trying to accomplish something they want to do. An error is not a sign that a child is defective (especially when it is related to an arbitrarily and externally contrived curriculum). Rather, an error is a sign of something that the teacher should ignore, allow to pass, because it is something that could cause the child trouble right now. If whatever is wrong has to be done conventionally right now, then the child should be helped to do it—with no "post-test" and nothing entered into the child's record. What the child can do with help today the child will be able to do alone tomorrow. . . . And if the child cannot do it with help today, or if the child is not interested, then it should be put aside.

Yet not only do many teachers continue to leap on every slip that students make as if errors were contagious, but "peer evaluation" now threatens to make every child in the classroom a member of a "mechanics" morality squad. No one will get away with a misplaced comma or reading miscue. (And when peers in a classroom criticize, they are rarely able to help each other because none of them is likely to have enough experience. All of the emphasis will be on how badly things are done, with little possibility of help to do them better. Exclusion from the club will be mutually reinforced.)

Teachers will say, "How will children know they are learning if their work is not evaluated?" But children are only uncertain whether they are learning or not when they are engaged in something that does not make sense to them in the first place. Normally they expect to be helped to do things in the right way—when it really matters. Teachers will ask, "How can I be sure children are learning if I don't constantly evaluate them?"

But teachers are only uncertain whether children are learning when they and the children are engaged in "instructional activities" that make no sense to either of them.

There is always an alternative to testing and grading. Any teacher can tell if children are learning about reading over a period of a few weeks, just by comparing the kinds and quantity of things the child is reading now compared with a month ago. And learning about writing can be gauged even more easily by comparing this week's writing folio with that of the previous month. Even parents, who are frequently held responsible for insisting upon comparative evaluation for their children, can be shown that their children have progressed in reading and writing by such direct and convincing demonstrations as I have mentioned. Principals and other immediate authorities can be shown in the same way that the teachers who are in their domain are doing their jobs.

Administrators and bureaucrats insist on numerical and comparative evaluation because it is their job to make invidious, pointless, and misleading comparisons between student and student, school and school, district and district, and among students, schools, districts, and the inevitable bureaucratic "objectives." Their occupations depend on data. But they could be given their data in different ways. Different things could be counted—like the number of books children read or the amount of writing they do—computed anonymously or by sampling, without pillorying individual children or teachers for their own performances. There are standard methods of compiling demographic statistics about health, occupation, income, and— if we wished, educational attainment—without ever having to make individual comparisons or personal reflections. No one need ever know how a particular child performed on a particular test—a right to privacy that is not denied adults in many out-of-school contexts.

And finally there is the political issue. There is a widespread belief in government departments that teachers will not teach and students will not learn unless every aspect of education is monitored and supervised. Officials outside the classroom are believed to know better how to educate a child than a teacher who knows the child. Central authorities are expected to get a better standard of performance from schools than a locally elected school board—or by employing that board as its agent rather than as the direct representative of the voters.

The ultimate response to people opposed to the massive evaluation that infests education today is, "Don't you want children to learn?" No one should get away with a loaded question like that. Proponents of testing and grading should be challenged to demonstrate exactly how they expect evaluation to improve learning and teaching, and to avoid all the undesirable consequences. There is no evidence that external control leads to better teachers or to better learners. There is a wealth of evidence to the contrary. There is a simple alternative to all of the testing, and that is to ensure that no child—and no teacher—is excluded from the clubs of readers, writers, and independent thinkers.

### How does an effective non-evaluative teacher collaborate?

Earlier this year, at an informal reception at a private house in Chicago for participants in a literacy conference, I met a most remarkable teacher of Greek. Everyone was speaking English, but there was a pleasant Greek atmosphere in the room, in the books that were around, in the pictures on the walls, in the music that was playing, (and in the refreshments). The setting led me to reveal that I had once studied modern Greek but had given up because I felt I hadn't made much progress.

The Greek teacher took me in hand. She found some books that she knew I would understand, simple stories with interesting illustrations. We easily ignored all the other conversations in the room. We browsed through the books until we found one that I was comfortable with. Then she invited me to read the story with her—in Greek. If I mispronounced a word, she didn't worry. If I struggled to say a word, she quietly said it for me, in Greek. If I didn't understand, she gently suggested a meaning, in English. I don't suppose I read much of the book myself, but she made me feel that I read it all, without any stress of being evaluated, in a pleasant collaboration. She devoted twenty minutes to me, and when we had done, I was a member of the club of people who read Greek. I might not have been very proficient, but I was well established. I was able to enjoy the next book by myself. And I started to look for other Greek books that I could read (with the help of the authors and illustrators) when my teacher was not around.

The name of my teacher was Sofia—and she was seven years old.

# References

Bissex, Glenda. *Gnys at Wrk.* Cambridge, Mass.: Harvard University Press, 1980.

Bloom, Benjamin S. *Human Characteristics and School Learning.* New York: McGraw-Hill, 1976.

Bloom, Benjamin S., et al., eds. *Taxonomy of Educational Objectives: Handbook I: Cognitive Domain.* N.Y.: McKay, 1956.

Bogdan, Robert C., and Sari Knopp Biklen. *Qualitative Research for Education.* Boston: Allyn and Bacon, 1982.

Boring, Edwin G. *A History of Experimental Psychology.* 2d ed. N.Y.: Appleton-Century-Crofts, 1957.

Calkins, Lucy McCormick. *Lessons from a Child.* Exeter, N.H.: Heinemann, 1983.

Chomsky, Noam, and Morris Halle. *Sound Pattern of English.* New York: Harper and Row, 1968.

Freire, Paulo. *Pedagogy of the Oppressed.* New York: Herder and Herder, 1972.

Goelman, Hillel, Antoinette A. Oberg, and Frank Smith, eds., *Awakening to Literacy.* Exeter, N.H.: Heinemann, 1984.

Halliday, Michael A. K. *Explorations in the Functions of Language.* London: Arnold, 1973.

Halliday, Michael A. K., and Ruqaya Hasan. *Cohesion in English.* London: Longman, 1976.

Hanna, Paul R., Richard E. Hodges, and Jean S. Hanna. *Spelling: Structure and Strategies.* Boston: Houghton Mifflin, 1971.

Heath, Shirley Brice. *Ways with Words.* Cambridge: Cambridge University Press, 1983.

————. "Being Literate in America." In Jerome A. Niles and Rosary V. Lalik, eds. *Issues in Literacy: A Research Perspective.* Rochester, N.Y.: National Reading Conference, 1985.

Hilgard, Ernest R. *Theories of Learning.* 2d ed. New York: Appleton-Century-Crofts, 1956.

Krashen, Stephen D. *Writing: Research, Theory and Applications.* New York: Pergamon, 1984.

————. *Inquiries and Insights.* Hayward, Calif.: Alemany Press, 1985.

Leichter, Hope Jensen, ed. *The Family as Educator.* New York: Teachers College Press, 1974.

Lindsay, Peter H., and Donald A. Norman. *Human Information Processing: An Introduction to Psychology.* 2d ed. New York: Academic Press, 1977.

Mandler, George. *Cognitive Psychology.* Hillsdale, N.J.: Erlbaum, 1985.

McPeck, John E. *Critical Thinking and Education.* Oxford: Martin Robertson, 1981.

Mead, Margaret. *Growing Up in New Guinea.* New York: Morrow, 1976.

Miller, George A. *Spontaneous Apprentices: Children and Language.* New York: Seabury, 1977.

Popper, Karl. *Unended Quest: An Intellectual Autobiography.* London: Fontana/Collins, 1976.

Rosenblatt, Louise M. *The Reader: The Text: The Poem.* Carbondale: Southern Illinois University Press, 1978.

————. " 'What Facts Does This Poem Teach You?' " *Language Arts* 57, no. 4 (1980): 386–94.

Smith, Frank. "Demonstrations, Engagement and Sensitivity." *Language Arts* 58, no. 1 (1981a): 103–12. Reprinted in Frank Smith, *Essays into Literacy.* Exeter, N.H.: Heinemann, 1983.

————. "The Choice Between Teachers and Programs." *Language Arts* 58, no. 6 (1981b): 634–42. Reprinted in Frank Smith, *Essays into Literacy.* Exeter, N.H.: Heinemann, 1983.

————. *Understanding Reading.* 3d ed. New York: Holt, Rinehart & Winston, 1982a.

————. *Writing and the Writer.* New York: Holt, Rinehart & Winston, 1982b.

————. *Essays into Literacy.* Exeter, N.H.: Heinemann, 1983.

————. *Reading Without Nonsense.* 2d ed. New York: Teachers College Press, 1985.

————. *Insult to Intelligence.* New York: Arbor House, 1986.

Spencer, Margaret. *How Texts Teach What Readers Learn.* Victoria, B.C.: Abel Press, 1987.

Taylor, Denny. *Family Literacy.* Exeter, N.H.: Heinemann, 1983.

Torrey, Jane W. "Learning to Read Without a Teacher: A Case Study." *Elementary English* 46 (1969): 550–56.

Tough, Joan. *Listening to Children Talking.* London: Ward Lock Educational, 1976.

Venezky, Richard L. *The Structure of English Orthography.* The Hague: Mouton, 1970.

Vygotsky, Lev S. *Mind in Society.* Cambridge, Mass.: Harvard University Press, 1978.

# Index